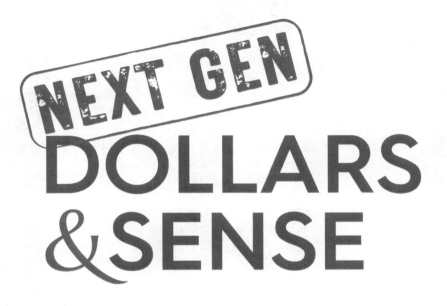

NEXT GEN DOLLARS &SENSE

By Joel Garris, J.D., CFP®, CFF

NELSON
FINANCIAL PLANNING

If you are a Nelson Financial Planning client, complimentary copies of this book are available by calling (407) 629-6477. Alternatively, additional copies of this book can be purchased on Amazon. Worksheets and videos relating to this book are found at www.NextGenDollarsAndSense.com.

The contents of this publication do not constitute legal, financial, accounting, tax, or any other type of professional advice. The views expressed should not be relied upon as specific investment advice or securities recommendation as individual situations may vary. Where discussed, past performance is no guarantee or indication of future results. All investments carry a certain amount of risk, including the possible loss of the principal amount invested.

Editors: Beth Wilson and The Team at Nelson Financial Planning
Cover Design: Erin Hamaoui
Interior Design: Jaimie Walter

For more information, contact Nelson Financial Planning at (407) 629-6477 or visit our website at www.NelsonFinancialPlanning.com

Nelson Financial Planning offers securities through Nelson Ivest Brokerage Services, Inc. a member of FINRA, SIPC & MSRB.

ISBN 979-8-35092-900-3 (2023 edition)

Contents

Preface i

Introduction v

Chapter 1: Human Behavior..1

Chapter 2: The Fundamentals 9

Chapter 3: Financial Goals 25

Chapter 4: Net Worth, Budgeting Basics, and
               Emergency Savings 31

Chapter 5: Managing Debt 43

Chapter 6: Credit and Your Credit Score.......................53

Chapter 7: Stocks 59

Chapter 8: Bonds 71

Chapter 9: Mutual Funds 79

Chapter 10: Annuities 93

Chapter 11: Rates of Return and the Economic Cycle....103

Chapter 12: Asset Allocation 109

Chapter 13: The Average Person's DIY Results 115

Chapter 14: Life's Big Purchases 125

Chapter 15: College Planning 139

Chapter 16: Taxes 147

Chapter 17: Retirement Accounts 163

Chapter 18: Social Security 179

Chapter 19: Death: The Other Certainty.......................189

Chapter 20: The Pitfalls of Inheriting Money................ 203

Chapter 21: Dollars and Sense 211

About the Author 221

Notes and Sources 225

Preface

  This book is 25 years in the making, starting when I first entered the industry and taught a personal finance course through the Orange County Adult Education Center. Since then, I've been privileged to engage in more than 40,000 hours of personal, one-on-one conversations with people about an almost infinite number of topics. But all topics really boil down to one thing—money: how to make it, how to use it, how to save it, how to control it, and how to spend it.

  In the next 25 years, more than $68 trillion of all that money will shift from one generation to the next—the largest wealth transfer ever in human history. With vast differences between the various generations in how they think, what they value, and the life ahead of them, now is the time to think about your personal financial plans and future decisions that may involve your loved ones. Take the time to have a conversation and share your thoughts with the next generation. While you can't take your money with you when you die, you probably don't want to see it squandered or fought over!

  That is the primary purpose of this book: to help not just you but, more importantly, your children and grandchildren understand the fundamentals of money and personal finance. In other words, this book is intentionally designed to help the next generation make sense of all of life's decisions involving their dollars—hence the book's title *Next Gen Dollars and Sense!*

  Despite the wide range of information sources available today (much more than when I taught 25 years ago!), individuals and investors are less savvy and more confused than ever.

This leads to the second purpose of this book: to help provide a practical perspective in a world flooded with social media, multitasking, and information overload that has spawned 10-second attention spans. Achieving financial results over time won't happen without more diligence, awareness, and focus. And let's face it—positive, significant results are rarely instantaneous; instead, they are achieved over time. After all, you don't reach that million-dollar target (or whatever your goal is) without starting with the very first dollar.

Third, as I watch my three sons grow into adulthood, their generation seems somewhat ill-equipped for the rocky road ahead. Entering a changing job market on the heels of a recession and historic pandemic, they now face soaring housing and healthcare costs, rising inflation and interest rates, and, for some, astronomical student loan debt. The days of pension plans are long over, and I would not want to guess what Social Security might look like when they retire. It is clear that any successful future retirement will become increasingly dependent on individuals personally accumulating savings over time. Yet this generation needs extensive education about and exposure to personal finance principles and economics. I hope that this book will provide the tools, knowledge, and perspective necessary for people of all ages to succeed on their financial journey.

Continue the Conversation

The concepts discussed throughout the book are not new. They have existed for decades and have been thoroughly discussed for more than 35 years on our long-running radio show (and now podcast) *Dollars & Sense*. The show still airs live every Sunday morning on various radio stations in Central Florida and was recently named one of the Top 25 Financial Planning Podcasts.

To subscribe or connect with our program, visit our website at www.NelsonFinancialPlanning.com or scan the QR codes in the About the Author section at the end of this book to access the show's various channels.

Acknowledgments

Many people deserve recognition, and thanks for helping create this book. First, thanks go to the good Lord above for putting the plan in place for this to be my career—one that I continue to enjoy immensely.

Second, I sincerely appreciate the thousands of friends and clients who have shared their personal stories with me, many of which helped shape the views and recommendations described throughout this book.

Third, I am grateful to the great team at Nelson Financial Planning for their help with this book. Jaimie Walter, Zach Keister, and Chet Cowart were the real workhorses for researching, writing, and assembling this book. Our team of Certified Financial Fiduciaries, Christina Lamb, Rob Field, and Kristin Kalley, along with Carolyn Grzan, Patty Theis, and Pilar Kalley, provided invaluable editing services.

Fourth, I want to thank my wife, Stephanie, a rock star in her own right and a source of great strength and encouragement to me and our three sons, who just make life more fun.

Introduction

Money is one of the most influential forces in our lives, bringing security, freedom, and happiness but also triggering stress, anxiety, and fear. Money is intricately woven into all aspects of our lives, from paying for necessities like housing and food to impacting significant decisions that affect relationships with family and friends. Managing your finances can be daunting and highly emotional, so learning about and making **SENSE** of life's decisions involving your **DOLLARS** is essential.

The first and most fundamental step toward establishing a solid foundation and achieving long-term financial goals is planning. Without a plan, it's too easy to get sidetracked, overspend, and fall into debt. But with this book as a guide, you will:

- Learn how and why to set financial goals, create a budget, manage debt, and build wealth.

- Discover strategies for navigating life's changes, maintaining financial success, and developing habits and mindset for long-term economic prosperity.

- Explore the essentials of investing and navigating life's big purchases, along with retirement, estate, and tax planning.

- Access valuable tools and strategies to achieve financial success.

Whether you're just starting your financial journey or ready to retire, this book will help you develop a solid plan for achieving your financial goals.

Chapter 1

Human Behavior

As humans, we are constantly bombarded with news and information. Unfortunately, most of it is negative. Why?

Well, as my good friend and longtime radio and television personality John "Bud" Hedinger once said to me years ago, "Well, you know Joel, negative news sells better than positive news."

He was right. A commercial news source or media company is not actually in the business of sharing information but in selling advertising opportunities. Focusing on the negative side of things helps retain and enlarge an audience. Increasing viewership allows a media company to charge advertisers more and thereby increase their profits. This reality sheds a very different light on the fundamental nature of the information around us.

The Role of Negativity

Negative news can have a profound impact on a person's financial decision-making. This is because people tend to react emotionally to any news, especially if it's negative, which can cloud their judgment when making financial decisions.

One study conducted by the University of Michigan found that people exposed to negative news about the economy were more likely to make conservative financial decisions, such as saving more money and investing less. This happens because negative news can create a sense of fear and uncertainty, which leads people to be more cautious with their money.

Another study conducted by the University of California, Berkeley, found that people exposed to negative news about the stock market were more likely to sell their stocks, even if it meant taking a loss. This is because negative news can create a sense of panic, leading people to make impulsive decisions without fully considering the long-term consequences.

Furthermore, negative news can also impact people's perception of risk. A study conducted by the University of Chicago found that people exposed to negative news about the economy perceived the risk of investing to be higher than those who were not exposed to negative news. This perception of increased risk can lead people to avoid investing altogether, which can negatively impact long-term financial goals.

Additionally, research shows that humans experience triple the amount of pain from a loss than they do the pleasure from a gain. In other words, if we lose $1,000, we feel an emotional response that is three times greater than our feelings about gaining $1,000. This psychological reaction can dictate our financial decision-making.

These and countless other studies have uncovered many cognitive biases that cause our minds to work against us and prevent our financial success. Cognitive bias occurs when someone interprets a situation based on their subjective opinion and personal experiences, which may not be impartial or correct. The rest of this chapter explores these behaviors and biases and how to prevent them from negatively impacting our finances.

Familiarity

According to the American College of Financial Services, our minds often use what we already know, or familiarity, against us when making financial decisions. This is because our brains are wired to prefer something familiar over something unfamiliar, even if the unfamiliar option is the better choice.

This cognitive bias can lead to poor financial decisions, such as sticking with a familiar investment even if it is underperforming or holding onto a losing stock because we are familiar with the company.

For example, far too many people held onto Sears Roebuck stock way too long just because they grew up with their Christmas catalog. Familiarity can cause us to overlook new opportunities or investments that could potentially benefit us in the long run.

To combat this bias, be aware of our tendency to favor the familiar and actively seek out new information and perspectives by researching new investment opportunities, seeking advice from financial professionals, and challenging your own assumptions and biases.

Anchoring

Anchoring is a cognitive bias that occurs when we rely too heavily on the first piece of information we receive about a topic. In the context of investing, this can cause us to fixate on a particular stock or investment, even if it is no longer the best option, leading to missed opportunities and poor investment decisions. To avoid the anchoring bias, remain open to new information and perspectives, and regularly reassess investment decisions.

In the late 90s, many people invested heavily in technology companies fixing anticipated Y2K concerns— potential catastrophic computing errors in switching from the year 1999 to 2000 (which wasn't accounted for when software programs were initially developed). When the calendar turned to the year 2000, and the world continued to spin, many of these same companies experienced dramatic declines as their products were no longer needed to prevent a catastrophe that never happened!

Oversimplification

Oversimplification is another cognitive bias that occurs when we try to simplify complex financial information or situations into easy-to-understand concepts or rules of thumb. While this may be helpful in certain circumstances, oversimplification can hinder your comprehension of financial concepts, resulting in poor investment decisions or missed opportunities for growth.

The reality is that every person is unique, with their own set of needs, wants, and desires. To avoid oversimplification, always seek out multiple information sources and perspectives and take time to fully understand the complexities of financial decisions before making them. We often see this oversimplification bias when it comes to retirement planning, as people forget to include their total healthcare costs or the impact of income taxes. At Nelson Financial Planning, we often spend several hours over multiple years mapping out a retirement income plan for clients approaching retirement.

Hindsight

Hindsight bias is the tendency for people to believe they could have predicted an event's outcome after it has occurred. This bias can lead people to overestimate their ability to anticipate events and underestimate the role of chance or other factors in contributing to the outcome. Hindsight bias is also known as the "I knew it all along" phenomenon. It can negatively affect decision-making when people make overconfident decisions based on their belief in a past event.

This is one bias that I recognize most often when talking to people at the office. They ask, "Why didn't you see this (name the event over the last 25 years) coming?" Sadly, there are no crystal balls or other ways to predict the future accurately and consistently. This behavioral bias can also manifest itself when people get out of the market during bad times and then try to get back in during good times. This results in selling low and buying high, which undermines investment results.

Endowment Effect

The endowment effect is when people tend to overvalue objects or investments they own because of a personal attachment. In the context of investing, this can cause people to hold onto underperforming investments or assets simply because they feel an emotional connection.

The best example of this is when people continue to own stock because their parents or grandparents once owned it, like General Electric. But the company is not the same as it was thirty years ago! After being part of the Dow Jones Industrial Average for more than a hundred years, General Electric was removed from the index in 2018 due to poor performance. To avoid the endowment effect, remain objective, take a fresh look at all available information, and keep personal feelings about a company out of your financial decision-making.

Status Quo

The status quo effect is the propensity for people to prefer things to stay the same or maintain the current situation. This bias can manifest in a variety of ways, such as resisting change or choosing familiar routines. Status quo bias can be a powerful force, as people often feel more comfortable with what is expected and may avoid taking risks or trying new things. However, this bias can also prevent people from making necessary changes or taking advantage of new opportunities.

To avoid the status quo effect, set specific goals and create a plan for making changes, which provides a sense of direction and purpose. If you are using a financial planner or advisor, make sure to meet face-to-face at least annually to review your account and make adjustments regularly. Many people struggle with change, but life changes every day, so why not use it to your investing advantage?

Bandwagon Effect

The bandwagon effect is when people favor a particular behavior or belief simply because others are doing the same thing. This bias is often observed when people are influenced by the actions or opinions of a large group of people, such as in politics, fashion, or marketing. The bandwagon effect can be a powerful force, as people often desire a sense of belonging and feeling part of a larger group.

However, these biases can also lead to irrational decision-making and prevent people from thinking critically about their choices. To avoid falling prey to the bandwagon effect, take time to consider the facts and make decisions based on objective information rather than simply following the crowd.

The interesting point is that the bandwagon plays a different tune nearly every year. From dot-com and meme stocks to crypto, by the time everyone is talking about something and on the so-called bandwagon, any potential investment opportunities are long gone.

As humans, we all fall victim to these behavioral biases at some point in our lives. My wife would say I am most susceptible to favoring the status quo and not as adaptable to change as I used to be. I sure do like my regular routine! So, how about you? Have you ever favored keeping the status quo? For that matter, how many of these basic human behaviors led you in the wrong direction?

Questions & Notes

Chapter 2

The Fundamentals

A handful of truths exist that are essential to understand and appreciate when it comes to investing your money and managing your finances. These are the fundamental building blocks for creating a successful financial plan and staying committed throughout your life.

As you review them, you may scoff at the seemingly simple words of advice that appear so easy to follow, but don't be fooled. As discussed in the prior chapter, innate human behavior and normal emotional responses can hinder even the most rational and diligent people from adopting the most straightforward concepts.

A favorite quote by Steve Jobs summarizes the importance of simplicity and the difficulty of achieving it:

"Simple can be harder than complex:
you have to work hard to get your
thinking clear to make it simple."

Ironically, you may need to reread that quote a few times to comprehend it fully. To help get (and keep) your "thinking clear," this chapter details the seven most important financial concepts that you need to follow now and in the future.

1. Time In, Not Timing

I can't begin to recount the number of people who have told me, "Joel, I am not going to invest now because of headline XYZ." Unfortunately for them, the market has proven repeatedly throughout its history that in the long run, getting into the market as early as possible, not at the best time possible, is what matters most.

Nobody can predict the future, but far too often, people wait to prepare or invest until they think the "timing is better." When this happens, they miss valuable earning opportunities and are usually forced into taking more significant risks later to make up for lost time.

Negative headlines and troubling events will always exist, providing a continual stream of reasons to put things off. Remember, though, that media outlets are in the business of selling advertising and negative news sells. Falling victim to the "wait and see" mentality due to the proliferation of pessimistic information is a distraction from achieving your goals.

For perspective, refer to the chart on the following page (courtesy of Putnam Investments), which reveals the pitfalls of waiting by showing the gains of not waiting. It demonstrates that if you had invested $10,000 in the market on December 31, 2007 (as measured by the S&P 500), you would have done so with perhaps the worst timing possible because the financial crisis in 2008 spurred a 39.6 percent market decline the following year.

Fast forward just three years for another memorable headline excuse to delay investing, which was continuously followed by multiple others:

- 2011—*S&P downgrades U.S. credit for the first time*
- 2016—*Brexit: Britain breaks with EU*
- 2018—*The U.S.-China trade war begins*
- 2020—*Economic fallout from COVID-19 continues*

A world of investing.®

Putnam
INVESTMENTS

Time, not timing, is the best way to capitalize on stock market gains

By trying to predict the best time to buy and sell, you may miss the market's biggest gains.

S&P 500® Index, 12/31/07–12/31/22

The U.S. stock market has been resilient throughout its history. Stocks routinely recovered from short-term crisis events to move higher over longer time periods.

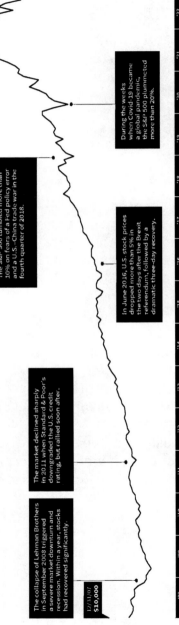

12/31/22
$35,461

The collapse of Lehman Brothers in September 2008 triggered a severe market downturn and recession. Within a year, stocks had recovered significantly.

12/31/07
$10,000

The market declined sharply in 2011 when Standard & Poor's downgraded the U.S. credit rating, but rallied soon after.

In June 2016, U.S. stock prices dropped more than 5% in the two days after the Brexit referendum, followed by a dramatic three-day recovery.

The S&P 500 tumbled more than 10% on fears of a Fed policy error and a U.S.–China trade war in the fourth quarter of 2018.

During the weeks when Covid-19 became a global pandemic, the S&P 500 plummeted more than 20%.

'08 '09 '10 '11 '12 '13 '14 '15 '16 '17 '18 '19 '20 '21 '22

Data is historical. Past performance is not a guarantee of future results. The S&P 500® Index is an unmanaged index of common stock performance. You cannot invest directly in an index.

Not FDIC insured | May lose value | No bank guarantee

These headlines are prime examples of when many people decided to wait to invest until the "timing is better." But the results speak for themselves.

Your time in the market during all these terrible headlines would have been richly rewarded. That $10,000 investment turned into over $35,000 in the fifteen years between 2008 and 2023!

When you stop waiting for better timing, you can instead follow the "time in" concept, invest earlier, and achieve profitable long-term investment results.

2. Pay Yourself First

Another simple-sounding concept that is more difficult to achieve is the strategy to pay yourself first. Far too often, people only save whatever is left over after paying all the bills. This nearly guarantees you will never save enough money because it's been relegated to an afterthought rather than a priority.

Instead, every time you get your paycheck, first set aside a portion of it for savings, and it's done! You are successfully paying yourself first. Even a minimal amount is better than nothing because it will build and grow over time, reinforcing the "time in" concept. Later, you can increase your savings amount as your income grows.

You can manage to pay yourself first by establishing a budget. We discuss budgeting extensively in Chapter 4, but for now, the pay yourself first strategy is critical to saving for priorities like retirement, emergency savings, and debt repayment.

Moreover, when creating a budget, recognizing the fundamental differences between your wants and needs is pivotal. Needs are crucial for survival, like food, housing, or healthcare, whereas wants are everything else, like dining out, new cars, and travel. You'll find that many regular expenses are wants, not needs. Putting a proper budget into place that prioritizes your needs and savings early in life will help ensure you get all your needs and wants in retirement!

Allocating a specific amount from each paycheck to savings eliminates any inconsistency, and establishing automatic transfers streamlines the pay yourself first approach.

If you are currently living paycheck to paycheck, consider earmarking the total amount of your next salary increase to go directly to savings. Then you won't get used to spending that extra money and can really get a jump-start on improving your financial picture immediately.

3. Be Consistent

This concept always strikes me as the most straightforward investing concept since being consistent means maintaining the same pattern of behavior over time. That sounds like an easy thing to do, right? After all, the human body likes inaction, and being consistent literally involves no extra effort. Consistency is like sitting on the sofa instead of running a marathon. Trust me, I've run marathons, and they are not easy! The only good thing about marathons in Florida is that the route is flat. Sitting on the sofa, like consistency, is much easier.

Another way to think of consistency is with the familiar direction to "just leave it alone!" You've probably said or heard it yourself at some point in your life and know just how hard it is to follow. Well, it applies to investing as well—leaving it alone is often best.

Distractions in a Disruptive World

When trying to achieve a financial objective, it's very easy to get distracted. Other seemingly more critical or urgent goals arise, shifting your focus to something else. This is particularly true with asset allocation, which is the precise mix of cash, bonds, and stocks utilized to reach your financial goals, which is discussed in depth in Chapter 12.

For instance, perhaps a few years go by after establishing a financial plan and something significant happens, like a job loss, a global pandemic, or a startling update from your social media. Suddenly, you feel compelled at that very moment to change everything. However, your plan was designed specifically to reach your goals over time and not instantaneously, so your most important role is to stay consistent and not get distracted.

These urges are intensified by the powerful devices tethered to us every hour of the day. With the average American checking their phone ninety-six times per day, it's impossible to avoid the latest distressing story. On many, many occasions, I have had phone calls with clients nervous about whatever disturbing current event is occurring. A considerable part of my job is providing a rational perspective in a wild world, so it's never the phone calls that bother me. It's the media frenzy and its harmful effect on my clients. The ironic part of these conversations is when I have to ask someone to turn down the volume on their television because I can hear the announcers in the background screaming at each other about whatever is going on and how bad it's going to be.

The fixation in the media and internet on all things destructive and outrageous messes with our minds and causes reactionary and usually poor decisions. That is why it is imperative to remain consistent amidst this barrage of inconsistent information!

Reactionary Decisions

From an investment perspective, making reactionary decisions can have dramatic consequences for your investment results. The chart on the following page (also courtesy of Putnam Investments) analyzes the same fifteen-year period from 2008 to 2023 discussed earlier in this chapter.

Stay invested so you don't miss the market's best days

$10,000 invested in the S&P 500 (12/31/07–12/31/22)

Stayed fully invested
8.81% annualized total return
$35,461

Missed 10 best days
3.29%
$16,246

Missed 20 best days
–0.17%
$9,748

Missed 30 best days
–2.93%
$6,399

Missed 40 best days
–5.32%
$4,401

$0 $10,000 $20,000 $30,000 $40,000

By staying fully invested over the past 15 years, you would have earned $19,215 more than someone who missed the market's 10 best days.

Data is historical. Past performance is not a guarantee of future results. The best time to invest assumes shares are bought when market prices are low.

For informational purposes only. Not an investment recommendation.

Investors should carefully consider the investment objectives, risks, charges, and expenses of a fund before investing. For a prospectus, or a summary prospectus if available, containing this and other information for any Putnam fund or product, call your financial representative or call Putnam at 1-800-225-1581. Please read the prospectus carefully before investing.

Putnam Investments | 100 Federal Street | Boston, MA 02110 | putnam.com

Putnam Retail Management

I508 332323 2/23

If you stayed fully invested for that period, your return would be nearly 9 percent per year. But jumping in and out of the market based on panic and fear could significantly reduce any gains. Just missing the ten best days out of the roughly 3,750 trading days in those 15 years drops your return by more than 60 percent per year. The accumulated impact of this performance differential is devastating to your financial results. When a difference of 3.5x more money in your hand is at stake—you merely need to be consistent and "just leave it alone."

Even more astonishing is that most of the market's very best days are clustered around the very worst days. So, all it takes is to react to a bad day, shift out of the market to "see how things turn out for a while," and your investment return goes in the toilet.

4. Be Diversified

Diversification is the act of spreading out your money across multiple asset types to reduce your risk and maximize your return. Because various investments perform better or worse at different times, you don't want all your eggs (or money) in one basket.

A diversified portfolio should have an asset mix consisting of stocks, bonds, and cash, providing flexibility when certain parts of your portfolio aren't doing as well. For example, if stocks are declining and you need money from your investments, you can access other assets like cash or bonds that should be performing better.

Balancing Risk vs. Reward

Diversification also means accepting a lower return than what the very best-performing asset class may be doing at any given time. That tradeoff is a necessity to minimize risk in any investment portfolio.

- **Riskier assets** may have better historical returns, but you could lose more money at certain times.

- **Less risky assets** come with lesser returns, but you lose less money during their worst periods.

It's the classic risk/reward tradeoff. The more risk you take, the greater the potential for reward, but also a greater chance of sleepless nights worrying about your money. Striking a balance is crucial to creating your proper asset allocation, which we discuss in depth in Chapter 12.

Diversification for the Long Term

The chart and key on the following pages (courtesy of MFS Investments) highlight the performance variability of different asset classes over the past 10 years. You should see that there is no discernible pattern of performance among the various categories of stocks and bonds. Each one, at separate times, had their day as the best-performing investment for a particular calendar year. This fact makes it impossible to anticipate which asset category you should own at any given time.

More importantly, chasing returns is useless at best. Far too often, investment products advertise their performance after a good year, so the money flows into that investment category only to experience disappointing results once it's there. We see it all the time.

For instance, look at the Large Cap Growth Stocks category on the chart on the following page. From 2019 through 2021, they were a dominantly performing investment. However, those who then concentrated their investments in that "hot" category wound up having a very disappointing 2022 when that category was the very worst performer.

In contrast, note the consistency of the Diversified Portfolio category, which represents an equal allocation among the various asset categories. It's never the best, but it's never the worst, which leads to more predictable and consistent returns over time.

Diversification Has Paid Off Over the Long Run (2013 – 2022)

Diversification, however, can potentially add value and help manage risk.

← Best — ANNUAL RETURN — Worst →

Rank	2013	2014	2015	2016	2017	2018	2019	2020	2021	2022	10 YEAR ENTIRE DECADE ANNUALIZED RETURN 2013-2022	20 YEAR WHOLE PERIOD ANNUALIZED RETURN 2003-2022
1 (Best)	Small/Mid Cap $136,797 36.8%	REITs $131,227 27.1%	Large Cap Growth $159,457 5.7%	Small/Mid Cap $167,234 17.6%	Large Cap Growth $222,325 30.2%	Cash $103,113 1.9%	Large Cap Growth $298,639 36.4%	Large Cap Growth $413,534 38.5%	REITs $259,224 39.9%	Commodities $87,869 16.1%	Large Cap Growth $373,967 14.1%	Large Cap Growth $772,283 10.8%
2	Large Cap Growth $133,485 33.5%	Large Cap Value $150,355 13.5%	REITs $134,232 2.3%	Large Cap Value $169,675 17.3%	International $146,250 25.0%	Bonds $110,964 0.0%	REITs $196,859 28.1%	Small/Mid Cap $269,532 20.0%	Large Cap Growth $527,732 27.6%	Cash $107,690 1.5%	Large Cap Value $266,320 10.3%	Small/Mid Cap $704,850 10.3%
3	Large Cap Value $132,527 32.5%	Large Cap Growth $150,904 13.0%	Bonds $104,392 0.5%	Commodities $63,230 11.8%	Small/Mid Cap $195,347 16.8%	Global Bonds $102,776 -1.2%	Small/Mid Cap $224,623 27.8%	Diversified $177,798 10.6%	Commodities $75,688 27.1%	Large Cap Value $266,320 -7.5%	Small/Mid Cap $260,026 10.0%	REITs $550,378 8.9%
4	International $122,778 22.8%	Small/Mid Cap $146,468 7.1%	Cash $100,112 0.0%	REITs $146,692 9.3%	Large Cap Value $192,860 13.7%	Large Cap Growth $218,960 -1.5%	Large Cap Value $223,871 26.5%	Global Bonds $119,903 9.2%	Large Cap Value $288,032 25.2%	Bonds $111,079 -13.0%	REITs $194,148 6.9%	Large Cap Value $542,806 8.8%
5	Diversified $113,415 13.4%	Bonds $103,821 6.0%	International $115,809 -0.8%	Diversified $125,542 8.7%	Diversified $142,121 13.2%	REITs $153,714 -4.1%	International $153,338 22.0%	International $105,861 7.6%	Small/Mid Cap $318,539 18.2%	Diversified $180,398 -13.6%	Diversified $180,398 6.1%	Diversified $397,816 7.1%
6	REITs $103,209 3.2%	Diversified $119,452 5.3%	Small/Mid Cap $142,219 -2.9%	Large Cap Growth $170,740 7.1%	REITs $160,287 9.3%	Diversified $133,623 -6.0%	Diversified $160,790 20.3%	Bonds $129,692 7.5%	Diversified $208,829 17.5%	International $157,873 -14.5%	International $157,873 4.7%	International $347,652 6.4%
7	Cash $100,050 0.0%	Cash $100,083 0.6%	Global Bonds $94,882 -3.2%	Bonds $107,156 2.6%	Global Bonds $104,024 7.4%	Large Cap Value $176,916 -8.3%	Bonds $120,636 8.7%	Large Cap Value $230,130 2.8%	International $184,543 11.3%	Global Bonds $95,694 -16.2%	Bonds $111,079 1.1%	Bonds $184,111 3.3%
8	Bonds $97,976 -2.0%	Global Bonds $97,972 0.6%	Diversified $115,467 -3.3%	Global Bonds $96,861 2.1%	Bonds $110,951 3.5%	Small/Mid Cap $175,808 -10.0%	Commodities $61,466 7.7%	Cash $106,048 0.6%	Cash $106,096 0.0%	Small/Mid Cap $260,026 -18.4%	Cash $107,690 0.7%	Global Bonds $170,985 2.7%
9	Global Bonds $97,402 -2.6%	International $116,760 -4.9%	Large Cap Value $144,600 -3.8%	International $116,968 1.0%	Commodities $64,308 1.7%	Commodities $57,076 -11.2%	Global Bonds $109,806 6.8%	Commodities $59,546 -3.1%	Bonds $127,692 -1.5%	REITs $194,148 -25.1%	Global Bonds $95,694 -0.4%	Commodities $131,210 1.4%
10 (Worst)	Commodities $90,477 -9.5%	Commodities $75,088 -17.0%	Commodities $56,574 -24.7%	Cash $100,383 0.3%	Cash $101,227 0.8%	International $126,081 -13.8%	Cash $105,436 2.3%	REITs $185,322 -5.9%	Global Bonds $114,260 -4.7%	Large Cap Growth $373,967 -29.1%	Commodities $87,869 -1.3%	Cash $127,335 1.2%

MFS®

43029.16   21

About the chart (chart key and risks on next slide): The historical performance of each index cited is provided to illustrate market trends; it does not represent the performance of a particular investment product. Index performance does not reflect the deduction of any investment-related fees and expenses. It is not possible to invest directly in an index. The investments you choose should correspond to your financial needs, goals, and risk tolerance. For assistance in determining your financial situation, consult an investment professional. For more information on any MFS product, including performance, please visit mfs.com. Past performance is no guarantee of future results.

The Diversified Portfolio: Equal allocations among the market segments are represented by the various market indices defined herein (excludes cash).
Note that the portfolio's assets were rebalanced at the end of every quarter to maintain equal allocations throughout the period. Diversification does not guarantee a profit or protect against a loss.

MFS

Chart Key

■ Cash[1]

■ Bonds[2]

■ Global bonds[3]

■ Diversified portfolio

■ Large-cap value stocks[4]

■ Commodities[5]

■ International stocks[6]

■ Large-cap growth stocks[7]

■ Small-/Mid-cap stocks[8]

■ REITs[9]

[1] The **FTSE 3-Month Treasury Bill Index** is derived from secondary market US Treasury bill rates published by the US Federal Reserve.

[2] The **Bloomberg Barclays U.S. Aggregate Bond Index** measures the US bond market.

[3] The **Bloomberg Barclays Global Aggregate Bond Index** provides a broad-based measure of the global investment-grade fixed income markets.

[4] The **Russell 1000® Value Index** measures large-cap US value stocks.

[5] The **Bloomberg Commodity Index** is composed of futures contracts on physical commodities.

[6] The **MSCI EAFE Index** measures the non-US stock market.

[7] The **Russell 1000® Growth Index** measures large-cap US growth stocks.

[8] The **Russell 2500™ Index** measures small- and mid-cap US stocks.

[9] The **FTSE NAREIT All REITs Total Return Index** tracks the performance of commercial real estate across the US economy.

International: Investing in foreign and/or emerging market securities involves interest rate, currency exchange rate, economic, and political risks. These risks are magnified in emerging or developing markets as compared with domestic markets. Small/Mid Cap stocks: Investing in small and/or mid-sized companies involves more risk than that customarily associated with investing in more-established companies. Bonds: Bonds, if held to maturity, provide a fixed rate of return and a fixed principal value. Bond funds will fluctuate and, when redeemed, may be worth more or less than their original cost.

Commodity: Commodity-related investments can be more volatile than investments in equity securities or debt instruments and can be affected by changes in overall market movements, commodity index volatility, changes in interest rates, currency fluctuations, or factors affecting a particular industry or commodity, and demand/supply imbalances in the market for the commodity. Events that affect the financial services sector may have a significant adverse effect on the portfolio. Real Estate: Real estate-related investments can be volatile because of general, regional, and local economic conditions; fluctuations in interest rates and property tax rates; shifts in zoning laws, environmental regulation and other governmental actions; increased operation expenses; lack of availability of mortgage funds; losses due to natural disasters; changes in property values and rental rates; overbuilding; losses due to casualty or condemnation, cash flows; the management skill and creditworthiness of the REIT manager, and other factors.

43029.16   22

5. Ignore Your Neighbor

It may be noble to "love thy neighbor," but chances are you probably want to ignore what they are doing when it comes to money, finances, and possessions. After all, looks can be very deceiving.

Your neighbor may have a big house, but that can come with a big mortgage, too. Those fancy cars in the driveway also could have expensive loans. Throw in credit cards that finance their fabulous travels, and your neighbor's financial picture looks a bit like a house of cards. Any changes, such as the loss of a job, medical issues, or an accident, and their whole false sense of financial security collapses—immediately.

Unfortunately, as humans, we are highly emotional beings who succumb easily to peer pressure, cultural expectations, and wanting to keep up with the Joneses. We all have a desire for approval, respect, and acceptance by our family and friends.

You might be surprised, however, by the actual statistics and characteristics of people who are millionaires (and those who aren't). The numbers paint a realistic picture of financial success that is very different from what many people view in their minds.

A Case in Point: Real Millionaires

In 2019, financial radio personality Dave Ramsey and his company Ramsey Solutions compiled the broadest analysis to date of millionaires, their lifestyles, and how they achieved their financial success. They found that:

- Eighty-five percent were hard-working individuals with regular jobs.
- One-third never made six figures in a single working year.
- Another third averaged about $100,000 a year throughout their career.

Not exactly a bunch of doctors, lawyers, and CEOs! Almost 80 percent received zero inheritance and did not grow up in upper- or upper-middle-class homes. They also didn't attend expensive, fancy colleges.

- 62 percent attended public state schools.
- 8 percent attended community college.
- 9 percent never graduated college at all.

The key finding? A staggering 94 percent of millionaires *live on less money than they make*, compared to 55 percent of the general population. Basically, almost all millionaires earn more than they spend to live—a critical concept known as *living within your means.*

The survey also found that the top two contributing factors to becoming wealthy were discipline and consistency. As you might imagine, only 7 percent of millionaires felt pressure to keep up with their friends and families.

6. Compounding: A Mathematical Wonder

When it comes to saving and investing, many people focus on return. "What's the rate of return for this particular investment?" they ask. Indeed, the rate of return is important, but there's a far more powerful force at play with what those rates of return can produce over time: compounding.

The power of compounding is described by many as a mathematical wonder. Compounding is applying the rate of return not just to the original amount invested but also to the profit that accumulates and reinvests each year. As that underlying amount grows, the profit generated grows as well, allowing your money to build on itself exponentially over time.

Here's how it works. Let's take a forty-year period, the typical timeframe people spend working in their lifetime. We'll also assume a 9 percent annual rate of return, which is in line with the markets over the past one hundred years.

Add in the rule of 72—a little-known mathematical concept that determines the time needed for your principal investment to double. To use this method, divide 72 by the annual rate of return. So, 72 divided by an assumed 9 percent return equals 8. That means every 8 years, your original investment, with the profit reinvested each year, doubles in value.

Successive doubling produces astounding growth. Assuming you invest $1,000 at twenty-five with a 9 percent annual return, you can see the increases in eight-year increments.

- **By thirty-three**, that $1,000 becomes $2,000.
- **By forty-one**, it would be $4,000.
- **At forty-nine**, it's $8,000.
- **At fifty-seven,** it's $16,000.
- **When you retire at sixty-five**, it's $32,000. That's right – a 32x profit!

And that's just for one single $1,000 investment. Imagine how large the number would be if you invested $5,000 per year (roughly $400 per month) for the entire forty-year period. By the way, it's nearly $2 million! Doesn't that sound like a decent amount to retire on by just saving $400 per month?

7. Congratulations, You're Living Longer

That's right, you will live longer, on average, than prior generations. The average life expectancy in the United States today is around eighty. Just fifty years ago, it was about seventy. Of course, your actual life expectancy depends on a host of factors, such as genetics, lifestyle, and access to health care. But those extra ten years or so on this good earth obviously come with ten more years of expenses.

Even more dramatic is how much life expectancy increases once you reach retirement age. After all, at sixty-five, you have already managed to avoid what could have killed you in your 20s, 30s, 40s, and 50s. Consequently, the average life expectancy for a sixty-five-year-old woman today is nearly eighty-seven years old, and a sixty-five-year-old man has a 50 percent chance of living to eighty-four. That's twenty years of retirement; is that good news for you, or is that bad news?

This longer life expectancy requires you to plan differently than prior generations. Many of the traditional approaches to investing or rules of thumb about allocation worked well when people lived to seventy but won't really work when people live into their eighties. Frankly, longer life expectancies require people to understand their financial picture better and sooner than prior generations.

If you aren't prepared to live longer with the assets you accumulated while working, then your golden years may turn out to be quite tarnished.

So, how are you doing? Are you following all these fundamental concepts regularly, or are you skipping over some of them? At Nelson Financial Planning, we send our clients regular, proactive communications to provide perspective and encourage continued adherence to these financial fundamentals.

In addition, our weekly radio show and podcast, *Dollars & Sense*, offers the very latest economic and financial news, so we encourage you to listen and subscribe. The About the Author section at the back of this book contains several QR codes to connect directly to our various channels. For your convenience, our most popular platforms are directly accessible using this QR code.

Chapter 3

Financial Goals

Setting financial goals is important for a host of reasons. If you have a dream, setting specific goals increases your ability to make that dream a reality. Likewise, clarifying what you want to achieve provides a clear sense of direction, which can help you stay focused and motivated to accomplish your goals.

It's the same in business, where companies must set goals and objectives to ensure long-term viability. At Nelson Financial Planning, we set corporate objectives on a one-, three-, and even ten-year basis to measure our progress.

Additionally, goals help prioritize your spending by making sure money is used in a way that aligns with what you ultimately want to achieve. With specific targets in mind, it's much easier to stay committed to saving money.

More importantly, having financial goals and tracking your progress shows how far you've come, which is a great motivator for staying on track toward achieving your objectives. Overall, realizing your financial goals also improves your economic well-being, reduces stress, provides a sense of accomplishment, and enhances your overall quality of life.

Identifying and Prioritizing Goals

Goal setting is all about developing a vision for your future—that first step toward obtaining financial well-being and achieving your dreams. This involves thinking about what you want for your life and how your financial objectives can help achieve that vision. Some people imagine retiring early, whereas others want the freedom to start a business.

Crafting a clear future vision helps you stay motivated and make informed financial decisions in support of your goals. You can start by identifying what you want to achieve financially. When setting financial goals, asking yourself the right questions will help you think about what matters most. Here are some to consider:

- What are my short and long term financial goals?
- How much money do I need to achieve them?
- What steps do I need to take?
- What sacrifices am I willing to make?
- How will achieving these goals improve my life?

Types of Financial Goals

You can set many different types of financial goals because they are personal to you and vary based on your circumstances and priorities. The list below contains some of the more common, fundamental goals to consider.

- **Emergency Savings**: One of the most common goals involves creating an emergency fund that provides cash in case of an unexpected event such as a job loss or medical emergency.

- **Debt Reduction**: Paying off debt, such as credit cards, student loans, or car loans, can help save a lot of money on interest and improve your credit score. Therefore, it's another goal most people have at some point in their lives.

- **Retirement Savings**: Saving and investing for retirement is an essential goal to adopt as soon as possible because the earlier you start saving money, the more it grows over time.

- **Home Purchase**: Putting money aside for a down payment on a house may help you qualify for a mortgage with better interest rates and reduce your monthly payments.

Create a Plan of Action

Setting goals is a critical first step; however, goals without a plan of action are just words on paper with little benefit to your future vision. To attain your goals and objectives, they must be clearly defined, measurable, and monitored. Here are five tips for creating a plan that will help improve your ability to reach your goals:

1. **Make Your Goals Specific and Measurable.** Once you have determined your financial goals, make them clear and measurable. Instead of saying you want to save money, identify exactly how much you want to save by a defined date.

2. **Prioritize Your Goals.** Decide which goals you care about most and prioritize them accordingly. This will help focus your efforts and resources on reaching your most important goals by allocating money toward those things most valuable to you.

3. **Create a Plan.** This involves identifying the steps necessary to accomplish your financial goals, such as creating a budget, increasing your income, or reducing your expenses. It's essential to create a realistic and achievable plan instead of a lofty pie-in-the-sky dream. For example, you shouldn't plan

to save 50 percent of your income if you need 80 percent of it to cover your regular expenses.

4. **Monitor your Progress.** Regularly monitoring progress toward your financial targets helps you identify when adjustments are needed and stay on track. Just like the activity tracker on your smartwatch motivates you to increase your step count or get more sleep, regularly monitoring your financial progress reminds you to stick to the plan for achieving your financial goals.

5. **Celebrate your Success.** It's beneficial to take time to recognize your accomplishments along the way. Reaching financial goals requires time and effort, so it's helpful to acknowledge and celebrate your achievements. Share your success with your family and friends—it might motivate them to improve themselves as well!

Pay Yourself First

I wrote about it in the prior chapter, and I'll repeat it now. Paying yourself first is one of the most valuable financial strategies you can adopt. Too often, people only save what's left over at the end of the month, and often, they find it's not much.

Paying yourself first simply means setting aside a part of your income for savings or investments *before* paying your bills or other expenses. This doesn't mean you don't pay your bills, but you may need to reevaluate how you spend your money. By paying yourself first, you prioritize your financial goals and ensure you're making progress toward them every month.

Reaching Your Vision for the Future

Don't forget that setting financial goals is just the first step. Making a plan and taking action are necessary to attain your objectives. Without action, goals are just words on paper, but with determination and commitment, you can achieve the financial success you've envisioned for yourself.

Don't forget the old adage that obtaining financial success is a journey, not a destination. By setting clear targets and taking consistent action, you can make progress toward the life you want to live. One of the best actions you can take is to establish a budget, which is what the next chapter is all about.

Questions & Notes

Chapter 4

Net Worth, Budgeting Basics, and Emergency Savings

Net worth is a measure of an individual's overall financial health. It represents the difference between one's assets and liabilities. In simple terms, net worth is what you *own* (assets) minus what you *owe* (liabilities).

Knowing your net worth is important because it clarifies your overall financial picture and shares insights on the areas that need the most improvement. Calculating your net worth annually and tracking it from year to year will show you the progress you are making toward achieving your financial goals.

Calculating Net Worth

To calculate your net worth, total all your assets and subtract all your liabilities. Assets are anything you own of value, such as cash, investments, real estate, and personal property. Liabilities are anything for which you owe money, such as credit card debt, student loans, mortgages, and car loans. The next page outlines steps to specifically calculate your own net worth.

List Your Assets

Start by writing down all your assets and their

estimated values, including:

- Cash and savings accounts
- Investments (stocks, bonds, and mutual funds)
- Retirement accounts (401(k)s and IRAs)
- Real estate (residence and rental properties)
- Personal property (cars, jewelry, and artwork)

List Your Liabilities

Next, list all your liabilities and their outstanding balances. This can include:

- Mortgages and home equity loans
- Car loans
- Credit card debt
- Student loans
- Personal loans

Calculate Your Net Worth

Finally, subtract your total liabilities from your total assets to calculate your net worth. For example, if your total assets are $500,000 and your total liabilities are $200,000, your net worth is $300,000. You can scan the QR code below to use our online net worth worksheet and update it every year to track your progress.

Net Worth Worksheet

Types of Net Worth

There are four main types of net worth that are important to understand.

Liquid Net Worth

This concept measures an individual's financial flexibility. It refers to the portion of one's net worth made up of liquid assets, such as cash, savings accounts, and investments that are easily converted into cash. Liquid net worth is especially important because it can help you quickly respond to unexpected expenses or life events.

Negative Net Worth

Stay away from this one! If you have a negative net worth, your liabilities exceed your assets. This means you *owe* more than you *own*. Negative net worth is a sign of financial distress and requires your immediate attention to avoid further financial problems.

High Net Worth

This is the one to strive for! Someone with a significant amount of assets is considered a high-net-worth individual. While there is no set definition for achieving this threshold, it generally includes individuals with a net worth of $1 million or more.

Ultra-high Net Worth

This refers to individuals or families with a net worth of $30 million or more and is a term often used in the world of wealth management and private banking. These individuals typically have a wide variety of assets and businesses that create a more complex financial picture.

Why Net Worth Matters

Knowing your net worth can help you make better financial decisions. For example, if your net worth is negative, you may need to focus on paying off debt and building up your savings. If your net worth is positive, you may have more flexibility to invest in your future, such as buying a home or starting a business.

Tracking your net worth over time can also help you see how your financial situation is changing.

- **Is your net worth increasing?** If so, you're making progress toward your financial goals.

- **Is your net worth decreasing?** You may need to reevaluate spending and saving habits.

Budgeting Basics

Budgeting is the foundation of any successful financial plan and is the single best tool to help achieve your financial goals. This process of creating a plan for your income and expenses allows you to make informed decisions about your money. In this section, we will cover the basics of budgeting, including:

- The importance of budgeting
- How to create a budget
- Tips for sticking to a budget
- Common budgeting mistakes to avoid

Fortunately, today's world offers smartphones and budgeting applications at your fingertips, making it easier than ever to record your expenses and keep your budget on track.

The Importance of Budgeting

Budgeting is important for several reasons:

- Helps you achieve your financial goals
- Provides a clear picture of your financial situation
- Reduces financial stress
- Helps avoid debt
- Improves your spending habits

Money is a highly emotional topic, but a clear budget helps you feel more in control of your finances. The mere act of tracking expenses helps you understand and appreciate where and how you spend your money.

It can be very eye-opening to see how much one can spend each month on regular Starbucks trips! Understandably, this example is a bit of a stereotype, but it does help to drive the point home about how the cost of recurrent, unnecessary spending habits adds up quickly.

Creating a Budget

The best way to create a budget is to do whatever works best for you—there is no right or wrong approach. Every person thinks differently, so their budgeting approach will differ as well. Here are some general principles to start creating an effective budget:

Start With Your Income

To create a budget, you need to know how much money you have coming in each month. This includes your salary, freelance or side income, and any other sources of income such as rental properties or other businesses. If you are retired, your income would include social security, pensions, and any other regular forms of retirement income.

List Your Expenses

Next, list all your monthly expenses, including both fixed and variable expenses.

- **Fixed Expenses:** These expenses are usually the same amount every month and are the backbone of your budget. You must make sure to have enough money to cover them every month. Examples of fixed expenses include rent or mortgage payments, utilities, and insurance.

- **Variable Expenses:** These expenses change every month based on your circumstances, such as groceries, transportation, and entertainment. Variable expenses offer more opportunities to adjust or prioritize your spending to save money or meet a financial goal. It may take a few months to get a handle on estimating your variable expenses but keep trying!

Don't forget expenses like income taxes and healthcare costs. If you are retired, make sure to include the money you spend during your free time (all those activities you now get to do in your free time generally cost money).

Categorize Your Expenses

It's important to also categorize your expenses into *needs* and *wants*. Needs are essential expenses that you must pay, while wants are discretionary expenses you can live without. Your electric bill is an example of a need, while an entertainment streaming service is a want. Make sure to allocate money toward your *needs* first and then your *wants,* as well as making sure you pay yourself first (this won't be the last time I refer to this strategy). Making this distinction will help you better understand how and where you can adjust your current spending.

Track Your Expenses

Tracking your expenses throughout the month is essential to ensure you stay within your budget.

Budgeting apps and spreadsheets can help keep track of your spending and are available on many different platforms. Even the technology available on a typical smartphone offers incredible budgeting and tracking capabilities.

The mere act of tracking expenses for a few months often helps people understand just how much money they waste. Between the ease of convenience, monthly subscriptions, and a host of impulse purchases—that Amazon habit is just one example of expenses that eat away at your future financial security!

Adjust Your Budget as Needed

Life is unpredictable, so it's important to adjust your budget as needed. If you are consistently overspending in a certain category, consider adjusting your budget or finding ways to reduce your expenses.

Scan the QR code below to download a budget spreadsheet we use with our clients at Nelson Financial Planning. You can use our template to track your own expenses.

Tips for Budgeting

Budgeting is a tool to achieve your financial goals and gain control over your finances. The key is to find a budgeting method that works for you and commit to your financial plan over time. This section outlines a few tips for making and sticking to a budget a little easier.

The 50/30/20 Rule

A budget should ideally be broken down into percentages, which helps allocate income to ensure you are not spending too much in any given area.

To calculate a percentage, take each expense category amount (like housing, entertainment, etc.) and divide it by your total gross income. Multiply that number by 100 to determine the percentage of income that expense consumes. While the exact percentages will vary depending on individual circumstances and financial goals, a common guideline is the 50/30/20 rule. This rule suggests that:

- **50 Percent of Income** should go toward necessities such as housing, food, and transportation.

- **30 Percent of Income** should be allocated to discretionary spending such as entertainment and hobbies.

- **20 Percent of Income** should be saved or invested for future goals and emergencies.

However, you may need to adjust these percentages based on your own needs and priorities. For example:

- **High Living Expenses** might require you to allocate a larger percentage towards necessities.

- **A Strong Focus on Saving** means you may be able to allocate a larger percentage towards savings and investments.

- **A Desire to Donate Money** to your favorite church or charity may justify carving out a certain percentage for regular gifting.

Ultimately, the goal of breaking down a budget into percentages is to create a framework for managing income and expenses in a way that aligns with your own financial goals and priorities.

Start Gradually

Even though a budget is the foundation of any financial plan, it can be tough to stick with it. One strategy to make it easier to begin and commit to your budgeting plan is to start in increments, like focusing on your grocery bill or entertainment expenses, and then gradually expand to other areas once you feel more comfortable.

Pay with Cash

Using cash helps tremendously when trying to avoid overspending. Simply cash your paychecks and divide the money according to your budget. Since most companies deposit paychecks directly into your bank account, you will need to withdraw the appropriate amount from the bank to get the cash in your hand.

The act of using physical cash actually increases the chance you will think twice about whether you really need to make a particular purchase—helping to limit impulse spending.

In fact, a recent neuroscience study led by Dr. Maria Ceravolo concluded that making purchases using cash instead of a credit card or smartphone enhances the negative impact of parting with money because of increased activity in the parietal cortex—the area of the brain that regulates your emotions. In other words, using cash causes stronger self-regulation signals to curb your consumption behavior!

Common Budgeting Mistakes

Budgeting is not an easy task; otherwise, everyone would do it consistently. The list below contains common pitfalls people encounter when trying to budget. Since knowing is half the battle, keeping these in mind will help you create and stick to your budget.

- Failing to include all expenses in the budget, such as recurring or one-time expenses.

- Creating an unrealistic budget that requires dramatic lifestyle changes or a sudden influx of cash.

- Living beyond one's means and spending more than is affordable.

- Spending money on things that are not necessary or don't align with one's goals and priorities.

- Trying to make drastic changes all at once instead of taking it slow and tackling a different portion of expenses within your budget each month.

Emergency Fund

Once you have created and understand your monthly budget, the next priority is to establish an emergency fund as a financial safety net. This provides stability in the event of unexpected expenses or emergencies and is essential to creating a successful financial plan.

The Basics of an Emergency Fund

An emergency fund is not something you invest; instead, it should be money that is easily accessible and without risk or volatility. Checking, savings, or money market accounts that pay some interest are typically used to hold emergency funds.

How Much to Save

The first step in establishing an emergency fund is to determine how much money you need to save. Our general recommendation is to save at least 6 months' worth of living expenses. This should include all essential expenses (your *needs*) such as rent/mortgage payments, utilities, groceries, and transportation.

Building your Emergency Fund

Once you know how much you need to save, set a savings goal to stay motivated and on track. Break your savings target down into smaller, manageable pieces to make it easier to achieve. For example, if your goal is to save $6,000 for an emergency fund, you could set a monthly savings target of $500. Within a year, you will achieve this incredibly important financial goal!

Emergency Fund Accounts

To make it easier to track progress and harder to spend that money on non-emergency expenses, open an additional savings account to separate your emergency fund from your other accounts. Opening multiple savings accounts is also a convenient way to earmark funds for different purposes, like a new car or a trip.

Make it Automatic

To make saving easier, consider setting up an automatic, recurring transfer from your checking account to your emergency fund savings account each month. This will help ensure you are consistently saving toward your goal (and paying yourself first) without having to think about it every month.

Stick With It

Building an emergency fund takes time, so be patient. If you focus on making regular contributions to your savings account and never use it for non-emergency expenses, you will find that over time it will grow and provide a sense of financial security and accomplishment.

Chapter 5

Managing Debt

Debt can be a valuable financial tool when used responsibly, allowing individuals to make significant purchases or investments they usually cannot afford to pay for upfront. Let me emphasize one word in that previous sentence—*responsibly.*

If it becomes unmanageable or misused, debt can lead to financial stress, missed payments, and a damaged credit score. Therefore, managing debt closely is crucial for individuals seeking to take control of their finances and achieve long-term financial stability.

When used appropriately, debt is a financial tool that can accelerate the improvement of one's overall financial picture. We don't recommend paying off all debt as quickly as possible, but it's essential to pay off your mortgage and any other debt before you retire. That way, you can spend money on activities you enjoy rather than sending it to your lender.

This chapter will explore the different types of debt and strategies for paying them off. We will also provide practical tips and techniques for managing debt, including prioritizing repayment.

Common Types of Debt

Credit Cards

This is debt accrued using a credit card to make purchases. Credit card debt often comes with high interest rates, making it difficult to pay off the balance. Credit card debt can be the most toxic because interest rates on outstanding amounts can be as high as 20% or more.

The most important thing to remember about credit card debt is to commit to paying it off in full every single month to avoid interest charges that dramatically increase the total amount owed over time.

Student Loans

This type of debt pays for educational expenses and can come from governmental or private lenders with varying repayment terms and interest rates. Student loan debt provides an important mechanism to help improve yourself and your financial future by obtaining a degree or other credentials that could lead to a higher-paying career.

Unfortunately, with the excessive cost of some schools these days, graduates don't always earn enough to justify their high-priced education. Students should take the time to conduct a cost-benefit analysis to ensure their prospective careers will allow them to repay their student loans efficiently.

For example, it's not a beneficial tradeoff to borrow $200,000 to attend a fancy college only to graduate with a degree suitable for a job paying $40,000 a year. If you want to pursue a career that generally offers lower-paying jobs, you could choose a more cost-effective college.

Personal Loans

These are loans typically taken out for a specific purpose, such as home improvements or debt consolidation. Personal loans can be secured or unsecured, and interest rates vary based on creditworthiness. The main difference between secured and unsecured loans is the presence or absence of collateral.

A secured loan requires collateral, whereas an unsecured loan does not. Collateral is an asset a borrower pledges to the lender as security for the loan and can be seized by the lender if the borrower fails to repay the loan. Some examples of collateral include a home, a car, or a savings account. Because of this collateral, interest rates on secured loans are typically lower than those on unsecured loans.

Auto Loans

This type of debt is used to purchase a vehicle, and like personal loans, it can be secured or unsecured with interest rates that vary based on creditworthiness. However, buying new cars every few years can hinder real progress toward improving your finances. New cars are expensive, and always wanting to own the latest model with its bells and whistles significantly undermines your financial future. A car should be viewed as a mode of adequate transportation, not a status symbol.

Mortgages

These loans are taken out to purchase a home and have fixed or adjustable rates and varying repayment terms. When buying a home, saving money for a downpayment first is advantageous to obtain more favorable borrowing terms and avoid paying private mortgage insurance. Chapter 14 explains the nuances of mortgage debt and auto loans.

Medical Debt

This debt is incurred when an individual receives medical treatment that is not fully covered by insurance. Medical debt can be a significant financial burden for many individuals, as it often arises unexpectedly.

Debt Payoff Strategies

There are several strategies for paying off debt, but the best one depends on your individual financial situation. The first step is to create a spreadsheet containing all the pertinent information about your current debt, including the amount owed, interest rate, term, and minimum payment required. Once that information is documented in one place, you can better determine which payoff strategy is right for you. Several effective methods for paying off debt are highlighted below:

Snowball Method

This strategy focuses on paying off the smallest debt first and, when it is paid off, taking the money you were putting toward that payment, rolling it into the next smallest debt, and so on. This approach helps build momentum and motivation as your debts get paid off individually.

Avalanche Method

This approach focuses on paying off the debt with the highest interest rate first and then moving on to the one with the next highest rate. This approach can save money in the long run by reducing the total interest you pay. It is our preferred approach to paying off debt because eliminating the higher rates first saves money over time.

Balance Transfer

Transferring debt from a high-interest credit card to another offering a lower interest rate helps reduce the interest you will owe, which can be an effective strategy if managed very closely.

However, these lower interest rate offers typically only apply for a specific period, and once that period is over, they're replaced with a much higher rate. It's essential to be extremely careful when playing this transfer game because any balance remaining after the special low rate ends will incur a much higher interest rate. In my 20s, I played this balance transfer game and got caught a couple of times not fully paying the balances off before the time expired. The additional cost of that higher interest rate usually negated the cost savings of the original balance transfer!

Debt Consolidation

This strategy involves taking out a loan to pay off multiple debts. By consolidating debt, you can focus on one monthly payment and perhaps even receive a lower interest rate. However, debt consolidation has a variety of drawbacks:

- **Higher Interest Rate:** If the borrower's credit score has decreased since they first incurred their original debt, they may not qualify for a lower interest rate on a consolidation loan.

- **Fees:** Some consolidation loans include fees, increasing the overall cost of the loan.

- **False Security:** Debt consolidation can also give the borrower a false sense of financial security, leading them to accrue more debt in the future.

- **Unresolved Issues:** Consolidating debt may not address the underlying issues that initially led to the debt problem, and without resolving those concerns, the borrower may end up in debt again.

Increase your income

Taking on a side hustle or finding other ways to increase your income can provide extra money to pay off your debt faster. If you want to get out of debt, consider taking that extra shift at work or trying for that promotion. Investing in yourself by learning new skills or obtaining new credentials or certifications could boost your work income. Lastly, ask your boss what additional skills your employer might need. Who knows, they might even pay for it!

No matter how you pay off your debt, it's crucial to create a plan and stick to it. Avoid taking on new debt and prioritize paying off debts with the highest interest rates first. With dedication and perseverance, you can pay off your debt and eliminate one of life's significant stresses.

Avoiding Debt

Accumulating burdensome debt substantially threatens your current and future financial security. One of the most common reasons people get into debt is because they spend more money than they earn. This often happens when people use credit cards to make purchases they can't afford or when they live beyond their means.

Sticking to the budget you made in Chapter 4 can help you avoid falling into debt because of overspending, and an emergency savings fund is critical to prevent racking up unexpected debt.

Additionally, high-interest credit card debt quickly piles up and becomes unmanageable if you only make minimum payments. It's best to avoid using them entirely, but if you are considering applying for a loan or credit card, examine the interest rates closely and refer to a comparison website to find one that best fits your needs.

Debt Negotiation

If you are struggling with excessive debt, negotiating with creditors may help take back some control of your finances. Before contacting creditors, assess your financial situation by calculating your total debt, income, and expenses. Once you thoroughly understand your financial situation, explain to your creditors that you need help making payments and request negotiation options. If the creditor initially rejects any negotiation, coming prepared to offer a compromise, such as suggesting a lower interest rate or smaller monthly payments, may help resolve the situation.

When you reach an agreement with your creditors, get everything in writing, including the repayment plan terms, the amount of your monthly payments, and the plan duration. This will help ensure that there are clear understandings later.

If negotiating directly with your creditors becomes too difficult, consider working with a reputable credit counseling agency to deal with them on your behalf. They will devise a repayment plan that works for you and provide financial education and counseling to help manage your debt in the future. However, any formal debt management plan remains on your credit report for a long time, and many counseling companies are less than reputable, so be careful with this approach.

When I was in law school years ago and deeply in debt from student loans, I was involved in an accident requiring an ambulance ride that generated a $500 bill. Well, technically, it wasn't an accident; it was my creation as a 25-year-old on skis racing a friend down a mountain and not wanting to lose! Needless to say, I lost big time. When I hit a mogul and went flying, I did not stick the landing; instead, it struck me unconscious. I didn't have an extra $500 to pay for the ride to the hospital, so I called the ambulance company and negotiated regular, systematic payments of $25. After a few months, I had put a dent in the bill and offered them $100 to settle the remaining balance, which they promptly took. Negotiating a debt works if you are willing to converse reasonably with the debtor and follow through on any commitments.

Bankruptcy

Bankruptcy is a legal process that allows individuals or businesses to eliminate or repay their debts under the protection of the federal bankruptcy court. Since it remains on your credit profile for ten years, it is a serious decision that should only be made after carefully considering the consequences. Declaring bankruptcy is never a good option and should be considered a last resort. Unfortunately, after declaring bankruptcy once, you are far more likely to fall into that trap again.

There are several types of bankruptcy, but the two most common are Chapter 7 and Chapter 13.

- **Chapter 7 Bankruptcy:** Known as a "liquidation" bankruptcy, Chapter 7 utilizes an appointed trustee to sell the debtor's various assets to pay off creditors. Once all the assets are sold, the remaining debts are discharged, which means the debtor is no longer responsible for paying them.

- **Chapter 13 Bankruptcy:** Also known as a "reorganization" bankruptcy, the debtor creates a repayment plan to pay off their debts over three to five years. The debtor gets to keep their assets but must make regular payments towards their debts.

Only some people are eligible for bankruptcy. To file for Chapter 7 bankruptcy, the debtor must pass a means test, which compares their income to the median income in their state. If the debtor's income is below the median, they are eligible for Chapter 7. If their income is above the median, they may still be eligible if they pass a second means test that considers their expenses. To file for Chapter 13 bankruptcy, the debtor must have a consistent income and be able to make regular payments toward their debts.

Bankruptcy can help individuals or businesses eliminate or repay their debts and get a fresh start. This process can also stop collection actions such as wage garnishment or foreclosure. However, bankruptcy significantly impacts the debtor's credit score and complicates approvals for future loans or credit cards. It may also affect the debtor's ability to get a job or rent an apartment. If you are trying to get your debt under control, bankruptcy should only be a last resort. A far better alternative is to follow through on one of the debt pay-off strategies discussed earlier in this chapter.

Questions & Notes

Chapter 6

Credit and Your Credit Score

Credit is the ability to obtain something before it's fully paid for based on the trust that required payments will be made in the future. Good credit is a financial tool that enables individuals to access funds for various purposes, from purchasing a home or car to paying for educational or unexpected expenses.

Your credit score is a numerical representation of your personal creditworthiness. It is used by lenders of all kinds, from large banks to landlords, to assess one's likelihood of making payments in full over time. Essentially, creditworthiness is how lenders determine if they trust you.

This chapter will explore many important aspects of credit, such as how credit scores are calculated, monitoring credit reports, and strategies for managing your credit score effectively.

Types of Credit

Several types of credit exist, including revolving, installment, and open credit.

- **Revolving Credit** allows individuals to borrow money up to a specific limit and repay it over time, with interest, provided they make payments on time. Credit cards and lines of credit are typical examples of revolving credit, and the amount owed each month varies with how much is spent.

- **Installment Credit** also involves borrowing a specific amount of money and repaying it over time, with interest, through equal monthly installments. Examples of installment credit include car loans and mortgages.

- **Open Credit** must be paid in full monthly and includes debit and charge cards. Unlike credit cards, charge cards typically don't have a preset limit but must be paid off in full each month. Any spending done with a debit card is automatically deducted from your bank account.

Good Credit

Good credit, or creditworthiness, is fundamental to improving your finances and offers numerous benefits, a few of which are listed below:

- **Lower Interest Rates**: Individuals with good credit qualify for lower interest rates on loans and credit cards, saving significantly in interest charges over time.

- **Easier Loan Approvals**: Good credit increases the likelihood of being approved for loans, such as mortgages or personal loans—sometimes with more favorable terms, such as extended repayment periods.

- **Higher Credit Limits**: Someone with good credit may be eligible for higher credit limits, providing more flexibility and purchasing power.

- **Better Insurance Rates**: Some insurance companies utilize credit profiles when determining insurance rates, so individuals with good credit may be eligible for lower insurance rates on auto, home, and other types of insurance.

- **Easier Rental Application Approvals**: Landlords are more likely to approve rental applications from persons with good credit, as they are considered more reliable and responsible tenants.

- **Better Credit Card Rewards**: Many credit card companies offer rewards such as cashback or travel points, but people with good credit often receive more attractive choices.

Credit Score

Credit scores are calculated based on numerous factors, such as payment history, credit utilization, length of credit history, types of credit used, and recent credit inquiries. Understanding how the different factors impact your credit score will help you better manage and improve it.

- **Payment History:** As the most crucial factor, one's payment history accounts for 35 percent of one's credit score and includes factors such as on-time payments, missed payments, and delinquencies.

- **Credit Utilization:** This is the amount of credit used compared to the total credit available and accounts for 30 percent.

- **Length of Credit History:** Representing 15 percent in a credit score calculation, this is how long someone has been using credit.

- **Types of Credit Used**: The variety of credit one has, such as credit cards, loans, and mortgages, account for 10 percent.

- **Recent Credit Inquiries**: This is the number of times a person has applied for credit, accounting for 10 percent of a credit score.

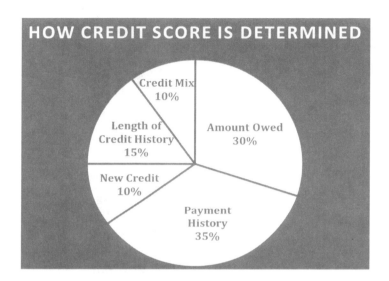

The list below provides the ranges of credit scores and where one would rank on the credit spectrum:

- **Poor Credit:** 300-579
- **Fair Credit:** 580-669
- **Good Credit:** 670-739
- **Very Good Credit:** 740-799
- **Excellent Credit:** 800 and above

We encourage everyone to know their credit score and complete these two critical steps:

1. **Know Where You Fit on the Scale Above**! If you aren't measuring up, read this and the previous chapter very closely.

2. **Review Your Credit Report** to ensure everything is accurate. Mistakes can and do happen, so make

sure everything appearing on your credit report belongs to you.

You can request your credit report from one of the three major credit reporting agencies: Equifax, Experian, or TransUnion. You're entitled to one free annual credit report from each agency by law, and you can quickly request your free credit report at AnnualCreditReport.com.

Since three different organizations track individual credit and provide credit scores, it's important to note that each uses slightly different formulas to calculate credit scores. Therefore, having slightly different scores from each reporting agency is not unusual. However, the factors used to calculate credit scores provide a good framework for understanding how credit scores are determined and are generally consistent across agencies.

Managing Credit

There are several strategies for managing credit effectively, including:

- **Pay Bills on Time.** Late payments can negatively impact credit scores and incur additional fees and interest charges.

- **Keep Credit Utilization Low.** Limiting credit utilization to less than 30 percent of the total credit limit is generally recommended. This can help improve credit scores and shows lenders that a person uses credit responsibly. For example, if your credit card limit is $10,000, keep your monthly usage to around $3,000.

- **Monitor Credit Reports.** Checking credit reports regularly can help identify errors or fraudulent activity and allow individuals to take steps to correct them.

- **Avoid Opening Too Many New Accounts.** Opening too many new credit accounts quickly can lower credit scores and make it more difficult to obtain credit in the future.

- **Use Credit for Necessary Expenses.** Using credit for essential expenses, such as medical bills or car repairs, can be a responsible way to manage credit. However, using credit for unnecessary costs, such as luxury items or vacations, can easily lead to debt and financial hardship.

- **Pay More Than the Minimum Payment.** Paying more than the minimum payment can help reduce interest charges and pay off debts more quickly.

- **Seek Help if Needed.** Resources such as credit counseling services or debt negotiation, discussed in the prior chapter, are available for anyone struggling to manage credit or debt.

Overall, having good credit can provide individuals with more financial opportunities. Maintaining good credit by making on-time payments, keeping credit utilization low, and monitoring credit reports regularly is essential since good credit is vital to achieving lifelong financial success.

Chapter 7

Stocks

Stocks are one of the four most common options in which to invest your money to accomplish your financial objectives. The following three chapters discuss the other common alternatives. Stock represents ownership in a company and is typically issued to raise money for expansion or funding operations. When you buy stock, you become a shareholder or equity owner of a small part of that company.

Your ownership of that company is based on the number of shares you own versus the number of shares outstanding. For example, as of mid-2023, Bill Gates owned about 103 million shares of Microsoft. Because Microsoft has just over 7.4 billion shares outstanding, Bill Gates owns 1.3 percent of the company.

Publicly traded companies are bought and sold on stock exchanges like the New York Stock Exchange, initially by selling their shares to the public through an initial public offering (IPO). The price of a stock fluctuates based on supply and demand, company performance, the current economic climate, and investor sentiment. When stocks are listed on a public exchange, anyone can buy and sell shares in the company, and its ownership is spread out among many shareholders. Because of this, public companies are subject to more regulatory requirements, such as financial reporting and shareholder disclosure rules. In contrast, private companies are owned by a small group of individuals, such as founders, management, and private investors, and their shares are not available to the public because they are not traded on any stock exchange.

There are a variety of corporate actions that can directly impact a company's stock. The two that occur most often are dividends and stock splits.

Dividends

Some companies pay their stockholders dividends, representing a portion of their business profit. These dividends provide income to investors and represent a portion of their investment return. A dividend also signals that the company is routinely profitable, willing to commit to a regular payout of its profits, and has excess cash flow to distribute to its shareholders.

A stock's dividend yield, which is the annual dividend income relative to the stock's current price, is a helpful metric for investors evaluating a stock's value. For example, if a stock is priced at $100 and pays a yearly dividend of $4, its dividend yield would be 4 percent. High-yield stocks include companies like Coca-Cola and AT&T that have very consistent revenue sources, whereas low-yield companies like Amazon and Google prioritize reinvesting profits rather than paying dividends.

Stock Splits

A stock split occurs when a company increases its outstanding shares by dividing each existing share into multiple shares. For example, in a two-for-one split, one share becomes two. Stock splits typically occur when the value of a company's stock has increased to the point where it is not affordable for small investors. Companies also use stock splits to increase their stock's liquidity, stimulate trading activity, and improve the marketability of their shares. Although a stock split doesn't change a company's value, it can signal confidence in future growth prospects, leading to increased investor demand and higher stock prices.

A notable example of a stock split is Alphabet's (Google's parent company) twenty-for-one stock split in 2022. Before the split, Alphabet's shares were trading at more than $2,255, and after the split, the shares traded at about $112 or 1/20 of their original value. In this split, each shareholder received twenty new shares for every share they owned. This increased the total number of outstanding shares and reduced the stock price proportionally, making the shares more accessible to a broader range of investors and enabling existing shareholders to accumulate more value over time by owning more shares.

Measuring a Stock's Value

There are various ways to measure the relative value of a stock and determine if it is worth buying. The three major approaches investors should utilize to understand the value of a particular stock include:

- Price-to-earnings analysis
- Quantitative and qualitative research
- Standard deviation

Price-to-Earnings Analysis

The price-to-earnings (P/E) ratio is a financial metric that conveys a stock's valuation by comparing its current market price to its earnings per share (EPS). A high P/E ratio may indicate overvaluation or high growth expectations, while a low ratio suggests undervaluation or lower growth prospects.

Comparing the P/E ratios of companies within the same industry or market segment allows investors to assess their relative value as potential investments. For example, if Oil Company A is priced at $10 with earnings of $2, its P/E ratio is five. In contrast, if Oil Company B is priced at $20 with earnings of $2, its P/E ratio is ten, double the investor costs for the same $2 earnings. The higher the P/E ratio, the more risk is necessary to obtain similar earnings on their investment.

Quantitative and Qualitative Research

Qualitative stock analysis evaluates a company's non-financial aspects, such as management competence, competitive advantages, and industry dynamics. Quantitative analysis, on the other hand, assesses a company's financial performance using metrics like market trends, trading activity, earnings, revenue growth, and valuation ratios. Combining both approaches provides a comprehensive view of a stock's potential performance and investment suitability.

Standard Deviation

Standard deviation represents the volatility or risk associated with a stock or portfolio by measuring the distribution of data points, such as stock returns, from the mean.

To calculate the standard deviation of a particular stock, determine the average annual performance of that stock and then compare the individual-year performances against that average. If the individual numbers are significantly greater or lower in magnitude than the average, this represents a higher standard deviation that indicates the potential for more significant price fluctuations and uncertainty.

Understanding a stock's standard deviation helps investors assess the riskiness of investments and make informed decisions when building a diversified portfolio.

Market Indexes

A stock market index tracks the performance of publicly traded companies representing either a specific market segment or the broader market. Indices help measure overall market performance and serve as benchmarks for individual investment performance. The three most common indices are described in detail on the following pages:

The Dow Jones Industrial Average

The Dow Jones Industrial Average (DIJA) is a stock market index that tracks thirty large, publicly owned companies that are reliable industry leaders, often called blue-chip companies. Microsoft, Coca-Cola, McDonald's, and American Express are some of the current DJIA companies representing diverse industries, including technology, healthcare, finance, and energy.

Created by Charles Dow and first published on May 26, 1896, the DIJA is one of the oldest stock market indices in the world. As a price-weighted index, the DIJA is calculated by adding up the stock prices of its thirty component companies and dividing the total by a specific factor adjusted for stock splits, dividends, and other corporate actions affecting the value of the index.

As one of the most reliable measures of the U.S. stock market, the DJIA often serves as a barometer of the economy's overall health.

The Standard & Poor's 500 Index

The Standard & Poor's 500 Index, or S&P 500, is a broader stock market index that tracks the performance of five hundred large companies listed on U.S. stock exchanges.

Serving as a benchmark for the U.S. equity market since 1957, it represents a variety of industries and sectors, providing a comprehensive view of the market's health. Often considered the most accurate gauge of overall markets, investors typically use it to compare their portfolio's performance against the broader market.

The S&P 500 is market-capitalization weighted, meaning its value is calculated based on the cumulative value of each component's stock price. Consequently, companies with larger market values have more influence on the performance of this market index. Market capitalization weighting can dramatically affect the overall performance of this index since only a handful of larger companies can dominate its performance during certain times. For example, from 2016 to 2021, the collection of five companies known as the FAANGs (Facebook, Amazon, Apple, Netflix, and Google) accounted for nearly 40 percent of the index's performance.

The National Association of Securities Dealers Automated Quotations

Also called the NASDAQ, this global electronic stock exchange is known for its prominent, technology-focused listings, such as Apple, Google, and Amazon. Founded in 1971, NASDAQ was one of the world's first electronic stock markets.

The NASDAQ Composite Index tracks the performance of all companies listed on the exchange, reflecting the health of the tech sector and the broader market. It also follows a market capitalization-weighted methodology using the latest real-time prices for the underlying securities comprising the index. It's an important benchmark for investors interested in technology and growth-oriented stocks.

The chart on the next page summarizes some critical distinctions between these three major indices. Understanding indices empowers investors to make informed decisions and gauge their investments' performance.

	Dow Jones Industrial Average	S&P 500 Index	NASDAQ Composite Index
Founded	1896	1957	1971
Number of Companies	30	500	2,500-3,000
Size of Constituents	Large companies only	Most of the largest US companies	Companies of all size
Nationality Constituents	United States	United States	Global
Calculation Formula	Price weighted	Market cap weighted	Market cap weighted
Known As	Most widely known index in the world	Barometer of the overall US stock market performance	Barometer of the technology sector
Type of Companies	Well-known large companies	Large companies	Mostly technology
Main Focus	Sustained growth	Financial viability, earnings	Fast growth
Sample Constituents	Walmart & Home Depot	Berkshire Hathaway & Mastercard	Netflix & Amazon

Exchange Traded Funds

Exchange-traded funds, or ETFs, are investments traded on exchanges in the same manner as individual stocks. An ETF also shares many characteristics with a mutual fund because these investments are organized as a diversified pool of individual stocks or bonds (Chapter 9 covers this in more detail).

Typically, ETFs are designed to track the performance of a specific index or a particular industry sector. Consequently, the individual component companies of an ETF are determined solely by their inclusion in a specific benchmark or sector. This static nature of an ETF means that its underlying holdings do not change, so it has low internal expenses. Much like stocks, ETFs can be bought or sold throughout the trading day at a market price that reflects the current value of their underlying predetermined holdings.

ETFs have become increasingly popular over the past few years, accounting for $6.5 trillion (or about 22 percent) of assets managed by the financial services industry at the end of 2022. Much of this increase results from ETF usage on financial advisory platforms, which are often higher-cost alternatives to traditional money management. Because of the lower underlying costs of ETFs, financial service professionals use them and layer in their advisory fees that often exceed 1 percent. Unfortunately, when combined with ETF investment costs, these higher advisory fees create a relatively high price for the investor that is not nearly the low-cost bargain the financial industry promotes when using ETFs.

Owning Stocks

Owning stocks offers investors the potential for profit through share appreciation and dividends, but it comes with risks. External events, such as changes in the economy, political events, or natural disasters, as well as internal or company-specific events, such as a change in leadership or a new product launch, can drastically influence the value of stocks and cause dramatic stock price fluctuations.

Risks with Owning Individual Stocks

The following list describes the various risks involved when owning stocks:

- **Company-specific**: Company-specific events such as changes in management, financial difficulties, or legal issues can impact company performance and cause dramatic increases or decreases in stock prices, depending on the nature of the event.

- **Volatility**: Stocks are inherently volatile, meaning their prices can fluctuate significantly in a short period, and their returns do not follow a smooth, linear path. This is due to a wide range of factors, including changes in investor sentiment and economic conditions. As discussed earlier in this chapter, volatility is measured by standard deviation.

- **Liquidity**: Liquidity refers to the ease with which an asset can be converted to cash. Stocks of small or lesser-known companies can be somewhat illiquid, meaning it may be challenging to sell them quickly at a fair price. This can be problematic if an investor needs to sell stocks to raise cash or to access other investment opportunities.

- **Currency**: Buying stock in foreign companies may expose investors to currency risk since changes in the exchange rate can increase or decrease the value of their investment. In addition, global companies selling products worldwide face currency fluctuation that can cause sales to appear more or less significant than they are. Changes in currency exchange rates can drastically impact a multinational company's stock price and the underlying intrinsic value of its sales.

- **Inflation**: Inflation is the rate at which the prices of goods and services increase, eroding the purchasing power of money over time. Higher inflation rates require a larger return to stay ahead of rising costs. Over time, stocks have proven to be the most inflation-resistant asset class because of their higher long-term returns.

As with any investment, owning individual stocks has several pros and cons.

Pros of Owning Individual Stocks

- **Potential for Higher Returns:** Owning specific, individual stocks can potentially provide investors with higher returns than investing in a more diversified portfolio. This is because a particular stock could outperform the overall markets at any time due to a company-specific event, such as a new product or service. As discussed in Chapter 2, diversification means trading higher return potential for reduced overall risk.

- **Control Over Investments:** Holding individual stocks gives investors complete control over their assets because they choose which stocks to buy, sell, and hold for as long as they want. In contrast, the specific companies within a mutual fund (discussed more in Chapter 9) can change regularly and are determined solely by the investment management firm offering the fund.

- **Ownership in a Company:** Owning individual stocks gives investors a sense of ownership and allows them to participate directly in the company's growth and success, such as voting on any material matter involving the company.

Cons of Owning Individual Stocks

- **Higher Risk:** Holding individual stocks can be riskier since the value of a single stock can fluctuate significantly in response to market conditions, news, or company-specific factors. Remember, a fully diversified portfolio will always have less risk than one concentrated on owning a handful of individual stocks.

- **Time-consuming**: Owning individual stocks requires significant time and effort to research and select respective companies to invest in and monitor their performance over time. The behavior of any company (and its stock price) is widely unpredictable compared to the broader-based market, which generally ebbs and flows with the overall economic cycle, as discussed more in Chapter 11.

- **Cost**: Holding individual stocks typically involves higher ongoing costs, including account maintenance fees plus trading fees applied to the purchase and sale of stock, which add up over time and erode long-term results.

Overall, owning individual stocks can be rewarding since stocks have historically generated better returns over time (but with more volatility) than bonds or cash. This approach provides more autonomy and control but requires careful research and monitoring. At Nelson Financial Planning, we believe owning stocks is vital to realizing positive long-term investment results.

Some of our clients (including one of my sons) like to buy and sell individual stocks using an online trading platform such as Robinhood or TradeStation. This is a great way to earmark a small portion of your portfolio for learning how individual stock performances work. You never know if you might find the next Amazon; if you do, it certainly makes for interesting conversation with your friends!

However, we don't recommend this approach for the majority of your assets because of the complexity, cost, and lack of diversification of just owning individual stocks. Consequently, our preferred method to accomplish clients' financial objectives utilizes mutual funds that focus on stocks. Mutual funds and our additional views are discussed in depth in Chapter 9. And yes, my son has invested far more money in his mutual fund account than in his stock trading account!

Chapter 8

Bonds

A bond, the second of the four main investment options discussed in this book, is a loan made by an investor to earn interest income and preserve capital. The bond issuer promises to pay regular interest to the investor and repay the loan's principal amount at a specified maturity date. This regular interest is the bond's stated interest rate or coupon, and the amount to be repaid on the bond's maturity date is the bond's face value.

For example, a bond issued at a 5 percent coupon with a $1,000 face value and a maturity date of July 1, 2030, will pay the bond purchaser $50 in interest each year and repay the original $1,000 investment in July 2030.

Bonds are issued by entities, like governments or corporations, to finance the construction of bridges, roads, manufacturing plants, or ongoing operations. Governments (federal, state, or local) issue bonds to fund public projects and manage debt, while corporations issue bonds to pay for business expansions or other initiatives. Bonds provide investors with a stable source of income and are crucial for funding public projects and corporate growth.

The world's largest issuer of bonds is the United States government, with over $24 trillion in outstanding bonds. The U.S. Treasury market is so significant that we review its history at the end of this chapter. On the corporate side, Microsoft is the largest debt issuer worldwide, with $64 billion outstanding at the beginning of 2023.

The bond market, valued at $300 trillion globally, is significantly larger than the global stock market, worth only $125 trillion. As a significant player in both markets, the United States accounts worldwide for about 40 percent of the bond market and 42 percent of the equity market.

Factors such as the issuer's credit quality, prevailing interest rates, economic conditions, and time to maturity determine a bond's price. Bonds are classified into distinct categories based on the type of entity that issues them, such as the federal government, local and state governments, or corporations.

- **Treasury Bonds:** Issued by the U.S. federal government, these are low-risk investments due to their government backing.

- **Municipal Bonds:** Offered by local and state governments to fund public projects, these provide tax-free interest on federal tax returns, making them attractive to investors in high-income brackets.

- **Corporate Bonds:** Issued by companies to finance operations, these are riskier than government bonds but typically offer better yields.

Bond Yields

A bond's yield represents an investor's return. If a bond offers to pay a coupon (or stated interest rate) of 7 percent, then the issuer is offering an annual return of 7 percent on the loan. A 7 percent bond yield indicates a higher annual return on investment than a 3 percent bond yield.

Higher yielding bonds often imply increased risk. For example, issuers of high-yield bonds may offer higher interest rates to attract investors because of concern that the issuer may default on future payments.

When an investor buys a bond at the face value of its original issuance, they receive the stated coupon rate. However, if the investor buys the bond after it has already been issued, the price of that bond may be more or less than its face value. The yield to maturity (YTM) then represents the effective interest rate earned by an investor who buys the bond at its current market price after its original issuance and holds it until maturity. The YTM can be more or less than the bond's original coupon, depending on whether it was bought at a higher or lower cost than its face value.

Bond Credit Ratings

Bond credit ratings assess the creditworthiness of a bond issuer. These ratings evaluate issuers' ability to meet their financial obligations, such as interest payments and principal repayment. These ratings, assigned by credit rating agencies such as Standard & Poor's, Moody's, and Fitch Ratings, involve a thorough analysis of the issuer's financial health, industry position, and economic factors. Ratings range from 'AAA' (highest quality) to 'D' (default), with investment-grade bonds rated 'BBB' or higher. Lower-rated bonds, such as high-yield or junk bonds, offer higher interest but carry an increased risk of default. Credit ratings provide investors with valuable information to assess the risk associated with a particular bond.

Interest Rates and Bond Yields

Interest rates play a crucial role in bond pricing. The current yield on a bond, or the effective interest rate, is inversely related to its price. When interest rates rise, bond prices generally fall, and vice versa. In a higher interest rate environment, investors have more options to obtain a higher yield on a newer bond, which decreases demand for existing bonds with yields based on a lower interest rate environment. This reduced demand generally causes the price of existing bonds to decline.

To understand how bond yields and prices move in opposite directions, consider the following example of a corporate bond with a face value of $1,000, a five-year maturity, and a 4 percent coupon. Based on the stated interest rate of 4 percent, the bondholder would receive $40 in annual interest payments. If the bond's market price is $950, the current yield is 4.21 percent ($40/$950), representing the yearly return an investor would receive based on the bond's current market price and coupon payments. In this way, a decline in a bond's price increases its current yield. Similarly, increasing a bond's price would decrease its current yield.

Bond Maturities

Bond maturities refer to the date a bond's principal is repaid to investors, ranging from short-term (one to three years) to long-term (more than ten years). A shorter maturity means that an investor is closer to the repayment of the loan and thereby has a lower risk of issuer default. Investors consider maturity when balancing risk tolerance and investment goals. For example, short-term bonds carry lower risk but potentially lower returns, while long-term bonds offer higher returns but increased sensitivity to interest rate changes.

Risks Associated with Bonds

As with any investment, bond ownership has various risks, including:

- **Credit Risk**: This risk is the likelihood that an issuer may default on interest or principal payments on its bonds.

- **Inflation Risk**: This is the potential erosion of the purchasing power of a bond's interest income and principal repayment.

- **Interest Rate Risk**: A change in interest rates can affect bond prices, potentially causing a loss if the investor sells the bond before maturity.

Owning Bonds

Bonds are an essential investment vehicle for a predictable income stream with lower risk compared to stocks, and every portfolio should have some portion in bonds. Generally, older and more risk-averse investors should have more bonds in their portfolio than younger and less risk-averse investors.

Owning individual bonds has similar advantages and disadvantages as owning individual stocks. With bonds, you know exactly what you own and can hold them until maturity. However, constructing a bond portfolio is costly, time-consuming, and offers less diversification when compared with the features of mutual funds focused on bonds, as described in the next chapter.

Treasuries

Treasuries generally provide a risk-free return because they are backed by the full faith and credit of the U.S. government, considered the most creditworthy borrower in the world. The U.S. government is highly unlikely to default on its debt obligations, and investors can be reasonably certain they will receive their principal and interest payments on time.

The yield offered by U.S. Treasuries affects financing rates from mortgages to cars and savings rates from CDs to money markets. When Treasuries offer lower yields, mortgage or car loan interest rates also decrease. However, this also means you won't receive much interest on your cash savings.

Long-term U.S. government securities, primarily Treasury bonds, have experienced significant fluctuations over the past 60 years. In the 1960s and early 1970s, long-term Treasury bond yields were relatively stable, averaging around 4 percent to 6 percent. However, high inflation in the late 1970s caused yields to peak at approximately 15 percent. If you bought a house back then, you would have been thrilled to have a mortgage rate of 12 percent! A gradual decline followed this period of high-interest rates and inflation as the Federal Reserve implemented policies in the 1980s to combat inflation and stabilize the economy.

The 1990s and early 2000s saw steady economic growth and low inflation, prompting further declines in long-term Treasury bond yields. The dot-com bubble in 2001 and the 2008 financial crisis led to temporary spikes in yields as investors sought safety in government securities during market turmoil.

In recent years, long-term Treasury bond yields reached historic lows, with the ten-year yield dropping below 1 percent in 2020. Mortgage rates similarly experienced a historical decline, briefly falling to less than 3 percent. Low inflation, low interest rates, and increased demand for safe-haven Treasury assets amid global economic uncertainties drove this decline. Recently, the Federal Reserve has raised interest rates to combat rising inflation, resulting in mortgage rates climbing to more than 7 percent.

A combination of economic conditions, monetary policy, and geopolitical events has shaped the performance of long-term U.S. government securities. These events and their impact on Treasury yields directly affect your finances because of their effect on both borrowing costs and savings rates.

Questions & Notes

Chapter 9

Mutual Funds

A mutual fund is like an Easter basket with candies and treats, from Cadbury™ eggs to yellow Peeps™ and everything in between. With a mutual fund, you own various companies in multiple industries that produce a cross-section of goods, products, and services that the world uses daily.

Mutual funds, the third main investment option that people utilize to accomplish their financial goals, are professionally managed investment vehicles that pool money from multiple investors and consist of diversified portfolios of stocks, bonds, or other securities. Shares of mutual funds can be purchased directly from the fund company or through a financial advisor, brokerage firm, or retirement plan.

The value of mutual fund shares is determined by the net asset value (NAV) per share, which is calculated daily based on the total value of the fund's assets minus its liabilities divided by the number of outstanding shares. Accordingly, the share price of a mutual fund is only calculated once per day after the market has closed and the prices of its underlying holdings have been determined for the day.

This chapter will discuss the features of mutual funds, their numerous classification types, their expenses, the general pros and cons of owning them, and how to analyze their performance in your portfolio.

Features of Mutual Funds

Mutual funds offer investors a variety of convenient, easy-to-use features. For example, a systematic withdrawal plan can be established on a fund to provide income at any time. Investors can pick the amount, frequency, and timing of these withdrawals and select options for direct deposit or tax withholding. If you are still in the accumulation or savings phase of your financial journey, a systematic investment helps ensure you invest regularly. You decide the amount and timing of the investment, and your contributions are automatically transferred from your bank account. Studies show that regular and systematic investing helps reduce market volatility compared to investing sporadically.

Additionally, mutual funds are easily converted to cash without extra fees, and redemptions typically appear in your bank account within two business days. Mutual funds provide investors with broad diversification without a significant outlay of money, as account minimums can start as low as $250. A typical mix of six to eight funds, like the type we use for our clients, would translate to ownership in about one thousand companies and five hundred bonds—a well-diversified and consumer-friendly investing approach!

There are several different factors by which mutual funds are classified, including types of investment holdings, company size, location, investment management style, future potential, sector, and target date.

Classification by Holding Type

Mutual funds are broadly classified by the type of underlying holdings that constitute their investment portfolios.

Stock Funds

Stock funds invest in stocks and own shares of different companies based on the fund's investment objective, which outlines the fund's goals and the types of companies it will invest in to achieve those targets. Investors consider a fund's investment objective a key factor when choosing a fund to ensure alignment with their personal investment goals and risk tolerance.

Bond Funds

These mutual funds invest in bonds, typically producing income for conservative investors or those seeking a consistent income stream in retirement. Bond funds can also be used for capital preservation by investing in lower-risk government bonds or, in the case of money market funds, cash equivalents.

Balanced Funds

These mutual funds invest in a mix of stocks and bonds, with a classic allocation of 60 percent stocks and 40 percent bonds. This mix provides bond income potential and stock capital appreciation while managing or balancing risk. We consider balanced funds a foundational part of any retiree's investment portfolio.

Classification by Company Size

The size of companies within the fund is also used to classify mutual funds. Market capitalization, or market cap, is an essential metric for grouping companies into large-, mid-, and small-cap categories, each with distinct risk and return profiles. Market cap is determined by the total value of a company's outstanding shares multiplied by the company's current stock price.

Small-cap Funds

These mutual funds primarily invest in companies with a market capitalization of less than $2 billion. Because smaller companies can experience faster growth than larger, more established ones, they offer investors the potential for higher returns. However, they can carry more risk because they may lack the larger company's product breadth or underlying strength. Small-cap funds best suit younger investors seeking long-term capital appreciation and portfolio diversification.

Mid-cap Funds

Mid-cap funds predominantly invest in companies with a market capitalization between $2 and $10 billion, balancing small-cap growth potential with large-cap stability. These funds are ideal for investors seeking less risk than small-cap funds while pursuing capital appreciation from emerging companies' growth potential.

Large-cap Funds

These funds invest in established companies with market capitalizations exceeding $10 billion. These companies are typically familiar brands that produce goods, products, and services we use daily. Offering relative stability, consistent dividends, and long-term growth potential, these funds may yield lower returns than small or mid-cap funds but serve as a foundational element in every investor's portfolio.

Classification by Location

The location of a particular company is another way mutual funds are categorized.

Domestic Funds

A domestic mutual fund primarily invests in companies and assets in the investor's home country. It, therefore, tends to involve familiar companies that broadly sell products within an investor's region. For example, a U.S. domestic mutual fund might invest in well-known American companies like Apple, Amazon, and Coca-Cola. In contrast, a domestic mutual fund in India might focus on companies headquartered there, like Reliance Industries, Tata Motors, and Infosys.

Investing in a domestic mutual fund offers growth potential as the home country's economy expands but limits opportunity if other parts of the world perform better. The performance of these funds depends on the performance of the companies headquartered in that specific country.

Global Funds

A global mutual fund invests in companies from countries worldwide, including the fund's home country. This strategy capitalizes on growth opportunities in different markets and countries, exposing investors to diverse companies and assets worldwide. Global funds typically contain a 50/50 split between domestic and international companies, providing global diversification.

International Funds

These funds expose investors to foreign markets and industries, providing growth opportunities and portfolio diversification beyond domestic investments. International mutual funds differ from global mutual funds because they exclude investments in the home country, focusing solely on foreign markets. Investing in international mutual funds carries unique risks, such as currency fluctuations, political instability, and regulatory differences. Still, they offer potential rewards through diverse economies and industries in other parts of the world.

A well-diversified portfolio should have a global perspective. While we are all familiar with brands in the U.S., many are owned by companies headquartered in other countries. Based on market capitalization, more than half of all publicly traded companies are domiciled outside the U.S. A fully diversified portfolio must invest a good portion in foreign companies, and we typically recommend about 20-30 percent exposure to foreign companies for proper portfolio diversification.

Classification by Investment Management Style

Active and passive management are two distinct investing strategies applied to mutual funds. With active management, fund managers leverage research and analysis to make investment decisions that seek to outperform the market indices discussed in Chapter 7.

Conversely, passive management tracks a market index, aiming to replicate its performance. For example, if a fund tracks the S&P 500 index, its holdings will include companies in the same proportions as their index. The holdings of such a fund rarely change—only when the companies within the index change. Hence, passive funds are often referred to as index funds.

Passive Management

Unfortunately, despite their appeal to many investors (especially their low fees), passive funds will never outperform the market index they track. Any expenses within a passive fund, regardless of the amount, ensure these funds consistently underperform their respective index. Let me repeat: *A passive index fund will always underperform and never outperform its respective index.*

In addition, without an active decision-making process regarding specific company holdings, an index fund will continue to own a company regardless of whether it is overpriced or performing poorly. While fund expenses are crucially important when comparing funds, an investor's net return (the return after expenses) is always the most valuable measure of their investment results.

Active Management

Active funds can outperform their respective index with potentially less risk; however, finding quality ones with reasonable expenses can be difficult. Between 1995 and 2021, an additional 4,300 actively managed funds flooded the market without offering much value to investors. These mass-produced funds typically underperform due to higher underlying expenses and less experienced portfolio managers.

A Final Word on Management Styles

One must be very careful about which investment management style is used by the funds they own. If an active fund is too expensive or performs poorly over time, a passive or index fund may be a better investment choice. Using index industry giants like Vanguard can be a reasonable solution for individuals lacking the tools or professional guidance to differentiate among all the options.

However, we at Nelson Financial Planning believe separating good active funds from bad ones is possible. We only consider active funds offering a twenty-year track record and a team-oriented approach to minimize risk. Utilizing these well-established, actively managed funds can help generate superior results with less overall risk for investors.

Classification by Future Potential

A company's growth management philosophy is another way to classify mutual funds. A company with a growth approach focuses on reinvesting corporate earnings for the future, while a value approach seeks to maximize current revenue streams.

Growth Funds

A growth mutual fund typically holds stocks of companies with demonstrated potential that reinvest earnings to fuel additional growth. A growth fund may include companies across various sectors or focus on specific industry sectors or company sizes.

Value Funds

A value mutual fund focuses on stocks trading at prices lower than the perceived value of the underlying company. These companies often have a stable financial position and typically pay dividends. A value fund may also focus on a particular industry sector or company size.

Classification by Sector

A sector mutual fund concentrates its investments in specific industries or economic sectors, such as technology, healthcare, or energy. By holding stocks of companies operating within a given sector, these funds offer targeted exposure to industry-specific trends.

Generally, we avoid sector funds because they restrict the pool of available investment opportunities by only holding companies in that sector. For example, your returns would be limited if you own a technology sector fund, but better investing opportunities exist in the financial industry.

Classification by Target Date

These funds automatically adjust their underlying asset allocation over time based on the particular year attributed to that fund, which represents an individual's targeted retirement year. Accordingly, the underlying asset allocation within these funds grows more conservative as the targeted year approaches by shifting to a higher percentage of bonds and cash and a lower portion of stocks.

Omnipresent in employer-sponsored plans, these funds often constitute the majority of investment options available to employees. Their use is widespread due to their simplified asset allocation: investors select their future retirement date (typically based on birth year), and the rest is automated. Unfortunately, hitting this easy button does not produce quality results, as these funds usually underperform the markets. In addition, to minimize any employer liability for investment selection, target date funds often become too conservative too early for the typical retiree. This is why we don't recommend target date funds unless your employer's plan offers no other options.

Mutual Fund Expenses

Expense ratios represent the mutual fund companies' annual fees to cover operating costs. Low expense ratios are fundamental to maximizing investment returns, as high fees erode returns over time. The lower the expense ratio, the more of the fund's returns you get to keep, ultimately boosting your overall investment performance.

Expense Ratio Fundamentals

To calculate the expense ratio, divide the fund's total expenses by the full value of its constituent holdings. For example, if the annual operating costs of a fund are

$500,000 with cumulative holdings valued at $100 million, then the expense ratio would be $500,000 divided by $100 million, equaling 0.005 or 0.50 percent.

Several factors contribute to a mutual fund's expense ratio, including:

- Management fees, which compensate the fund manager for their expertise

- Operating costs, such as administrative, legal, and accounting expenses

Expense ratios vary significantly by mutual fund, ranging from 0.5 percent to more than 1 percent annually. Index funds and ETFs (those stock-acting, mutual fund-like investments discussed in Chapter 7) have expense ratios between 0.25 percent and 0.75 percent. Index fund and ETF expense ratios are slightly lower than those of traditional actively managed mutual funds due to their pre-determined and static portfolios. An underlying cost between 0.25 percent and 1 percent per year is a wide range that must be accounted for when selecting a particular investment.

Tips for Selecting Based on Expenses

To optimize your investment strategy and minimize your expenses, consider the following tips when selecting mutual funds or ETFs with varying expense ratios:

- Compare expense ratios across similar funds to identify cost-effective options.

- Research the fund's historical performance to ensure returns aren't sacrificed for lower fees. Net performance after expenses should always prevail over anything else.

- Factor in other expenses, such as sales charges, transaction costs, and financial professional fees that impact your overall investment returns.

Understanding and comparing expense ratios and total investment costs is vital to selecting your underlying investments and creating an optimal financial plan to meet your goals. Choosing investments with lower expense ratios helps maximize your investment returns and make the most of your hard-earned money. To ensure our clients receive the best net return possible, we use investments that typically rank in the lowest quartile of expenses relative to their peers.

Professional Fees

If you work with a financial professional, their fee may be in addition to any investment expenses or bundled together as another component of the investment's underlying expense ratio. At Nelson Financial Planning, we utilize a bundled approach, as most investors forget to add together fund expenses and professional fees for an accurate view of overall investment costs. Even worse, many investors don't realize the existence of these two different expense components.

Take the time to understand your fund or ETF expenses and the financial professional fees you pay. If the financial professional fee exceeds 1 percent, you are spending too much! Sadly, we regularly see financial professional fees above 1.5 percent. Combined with mutual fund or ETF expenses, this cost can exceed 2 percent per year and significantly drag down your investment results.

Pros and Cons of Mutual Funds

Just like any other investment, owning mutual funds has a variety of positives and negatives associated with them.

Pros of Owning Mutual Funds

- **Diversification**: Mutual funds invest in various assets, reducing loss risk if an individual holding performs poorly. This diversification distributes investment risk to provide more consistent returns over time.

- **Professional Management**: Professional fund managers have the expertise and resources to research and analyze investments, which can lead to better decisions, particularly with well-established, actively managed funds.

- **Flexibility**: Mutual funds offer many user-friendly features, from the ability to make systematic withdrawals or investments to providing quick and easy cash conversions. These flexible options assist investors in efficiently using their money.

- **Affordability**: Mutual funds' low minimum investment requirements are more accessible to investors with less capital, underscoring their broad-based appeal to everyday hard-working Americans.

Cons of Owning Mutual Funds

- **Fees**: Mutual funds charge various management and administrative fees, which decrease returns and overall fund performance.

- **Passive Management**: Some mutual funds track an index, which means the fund manager is not actively making investment decisions. Similarly,

ETFs hold a predetermined and static collection of companies that represent a particular index. Remember, index funds will always underperform and never outperform their respective index!

- **Taxation**: When a mutual fund receives dividends or interest from its holdings or sells any underlying assets, tax implications are passed through proportionately to the owners of that fund. This pass-through tax treatment means investors must pay taxes on income or profit they did not direct or control. When mutual funds are used in non-retirement accounts, this reduces tax efficiency.

- **Lack of Control**: Investors do not have direct control over the securities held in a mutual fund, which means they cannot choose which securities are bought or sold.

At Nelson Financial Planning, we believe the pros outweigh the cons regarding mutual funds. Despite the potential for tax inefficiency in certain types of accounts, correctly screening for actively managed funds with consistent long-term investment results is an ideal option for a well-diversified, better-performing, and highly flexible investment plan.

Morningstar Analysis

Morningstar is one of the most well-known companies that measures and ranks the performance of various investments. A Morningstar analysis is a valuable, independent tool for gauging the performance and diversification of a portfolio as well as monitoring risk and allocation. Its in-depth independent analysis covers the full range of investments, from mutual funds and ETFs to stocks and bonds.

A Morningstar analysis helps investors make informed decisions with unbiased, comprehensive evaluations of different investment options and detailed analysis of an investment portfolio. This overview helps understand a portfolio's composition and risk by looking at asset allocation, sector exposure, geographical distribution, and individual holdings. Using Morningstar, investors can identify potential areas of concern, such as overexposure to a specific sector or insufficient diversification.

At Nelson Financial Planning, we use Morningstar every day to help monitor client performance, risk, and diversification. These analyses allow us to rebalance client portfolios proactively to ensure positive long-term results.

If you would like a free Morningstar analysis of your current portfolio, visit the Contact Us section of our website at www.NelsonFinancialPlanning.com and request your free Morningstar review. Better yet, scan the QR code below and request one immediately.

Chapter 10

Annuities

Annuities, another of the four primary investment options, are an increasingly popular financial product, with 2022 sales hitting $310.8 billion and surpassing the prior annual record from 2008 by 17 percent. The timing of those sales records—2022 and 2008—reveals the appeal of annuities, as both years coincided with dramatic market declines and rising investor fear and anxiety. This fear factor becomes the central theme of annuity advertisements during these times, causing investors to purchase annuities based on emotion instead of rationally assessing whether an annuity makes sense. The reality is that annuities are highly complex investment products with numerous features and fine print that people rarely fully understand. Far too often, we find ourselves explaining the characteristics of an annuity to an investor after they have already purchased one.

Annuities are insurance contracts offering tax-deferred growth, guaranteed income streams, and some protection from market volatility. When selecting an annuity, investors can choose from a wide array of features, each with an associated cost as part of the ongoing expense.

Annuity Contract Parties

There are four distinct parties to an annuity contract:

Contract Owner

The owner is the individual or entity purchasing an annuity from an insurance company and controls the contract, chooses beneficiaries, determines payout options, and makes withdrawal decisions. The contract owner must understand the terms, costs, and potential annuity surrender charges, which are fees for withdrawing money within a defined period after purchasing.

Annuitant

The annuitant is the individual whose life expectancy determines the annuity payments and cannot change once named. When the annuitant passes away, the designated beneficiaries receive any remaining benefits. The annuitant's age, gender, and life expectancy are crucial factors in calculating the payment amounts an annuity can generate. The annuitant and contract owner are typically the same person, but they can differ.

Beneficiary

The individual or entity designated as the beneficiary receives the remaining annuity benefits upon the annuitant's death. The contract owner selects the beneficiary, who may be a spouse, family member, trust, or charity, and subject to the contract terms, it can be changed as needed. Depending on the annuity contract's provisions and the owner's selected payout options, the beneficiary may receive a lump sum, installment payments, or a continuation of annuity income.

Insurance Company

The company issuing the annuity is responsible for ensuring the completion of the underlying contract provisions. Every insurance company is rated for its financial strength and ability to pay claims, which helps consumers make informed selections between annuity issuers.

Annuity Features

Annuities can have both life insurance features and investment-oriented characteristics. On the insurance side, annuities often have a death benefit tied directly to the underlying investment. In a typical annuity, when the annuitant dies, the beneficiary receives whichever is greater: the contract value or the amount invested. Because benefits are paid based directly on the amount invested, there are no health requirements to obtain this life insurance coverage. The owner can also pay for an additional death benefit under the contract. However, extra insurance features, known as riders to the policy, increase the underlying annuity cost.

On the investment side, depending on the type of annuity, the product can generate interest or have subaccounts that allow the contract owner to create a diversified portfolio. Subaccounts resemble mutual funds because they consist of various holdings of stocks, bonds, or both.

Annuities are tax-deferred products whose earnings grow tax-free until withdrawn and are fundable with after-tax dollars or retirement funds. If using retirement funds, the distribution rules of retirement accounts apply (this will be discussed in Chapter 17). In our opinion, it's illogical to use retirement funds inside an annuity because both offer tax-deferred growth. To use a bit of a throwback analogy, that's like wearing both a belt and suspenders: one is sufficient to hold your pants up, but wearing both seems unnecessary. We believe holding retirement assets inside an annuity is a needless duplication.

For annuities funded with after-tax dollars, only the growth on those dollars is taxable, but the growth is always taken first on any withdrawals. This growth is taxed at ordinary income tax rates like retirement account distributions, so if an individual under age fifty-nine and a half wants to withdraw money, a 10 percent income tax penalty also applies. Given this potential tax penalty, it doesn't make sense for someone in their 40s or 50s to invest after-tax dollars in an annuity.

Types of Annuities

There are three basic types of annuities: fixed, equity-indexed, and variable; however, all annuities typically include fees to surrender the account or access money, and depending on the annuity type, these charges can be pretty significant.

Fixed Annuities

These annuities provide the contract owner a guaranteed fixed rate of return for a particular period and then reset to a rate determined by the insurance company—usually much lower than prevailing interest rates. Fixed annuities appeal to those seeking safety and better savings rates than their bank offers.

Between 2021 and 2022, fixed annuity sales more than doubled due to a tough economic year, rising interest rates, and declining bank savings rates. Unfortunately, these products may look like a bank certificate of deposit because they offer a set rate for a specified period, but they are not FDIC-insured!

Equity-Indexed Annuities

These annuities have exploded in popularity over the past several years due to extensive and often misleading marketing. Equity-indexed annuities are essentially fixed annuities with a rider allowing quasi-participation in the market. Advertised as offering the upside of the markets without any downside risk, these products contain extensive fine print and restrictions that produce investor returns no better than a fixed annuity. Moreover, surrender charges as high as 15 percent that last up to fifteen years are more substantial than any other type of annuity.

Investors should be particularly wary of sales pitches for this type of annuity. Advertisements suggest this product increases in value when the markets go up but doesn't lose value when the markets go down. That promotion sounds great, but it's too good to be true. Without being able to predict the future, no investment product can access all the positive returns of the market without incurring losses during declines. Unfortunately, sales of this product continue to expand—increasing 8 percent in 2022 and claiming a record amount of investors' dollars.

Variable Annuities

These annuities offer different investment choices within the contract, consisting of stocks and bonds pooled into separate subaccounts, with the overall value based on investment performance. Because they are considered investment-oriented products with insurance features, variable annuity sales representatives must be licensed to sell securities and are subject to more intensive federal regulatory scrutiny and requirements. In contrast, as purely insurance products, fixed and equity-linked annuity sales representatives only need a state-issued insurance license and are not subject to the same level of federal oversight.

Income Options

One popular feature of annuities is the ability to elect a steady, defined income stream from the insurance company, as outlined in the annuity contract provisions. Any such guaranteed income option is based solely on the insurance company's ability to meet the promised contract terms. There are three methods an owner can use to receive money from an annuity.

Contract Withdrawals

Withdrawals from an annuity are permitted at any time. However, these redemptions may be subject to surrender charges if they exceed certain threshold amounts. These types of withdrawals do not trigger any contract guarantee since the underlying cash value of an annuity is utilized.

Exercise a Retirement Income Benefit

This contract rider must be elected during the initial annuity purchase, costing about 1.25 percent per year in extra expenses. While the payout of these income riders is guaranteed, the promised returns are often misleading.

An 8 percent return on investment is advertised, but this calculation includes the return of your actual investment. Despite what the annuity advertisements assert, that should never be considered a part of your profit. Your real rate of return (i.e., the actual profit on the investment you made initially) is typically only 2 to 3 percent.

Here is an example of how these riders work. If you invest $100,000 and utilize a typical income benefit rider, you receive 8 percent of that investment, or $8,000 per year. After twenty years, you will have collected a total of $160,000. However, the actual profit on your original investment of $100,000 is only $60,000 or the equivalent of $3,000 per year. This is a mere 3 percent rate of return on your $100,000 investment, not an 8 percent return.

Annuitize the Contract

The process of annuitizing means agreeing to a set income stream based on your age and the current value of the annuity. In exchange, you give up all rights to access the underlying annuity value. Annuitizing permanently converts your annuity investment into regular income from the insurance company, guaranteed to last your lifetime. This approach to collecting income is considered a last resort because of its irrevocable nature. In addition, the effective rate of return when you annuitize is low (2 to 3 percent), like that of an income benefit rider.

Annuity Expenses

With many underlying expenses, such as insurance costs and riders, annuities can be an expensive investment choice.

- Every annuity has a cost associated with its underlying life insurance features, known as the mortality expense. Ranging from 0.75 to 1.25 percent per year, it increases further if any extra death benefit option is elected.

- With variable annuities, each subaccount has underlying expenses ranging from 0.75 to 1 percent per year.

- The typical annual cost of the guaranteed income rider discussed previously is 1.25 percent.

After totaling all the costs, annual annuity expenses can exceed 3 percent per year—significantly diminishing investment results!

The Bottom Line

A significant factor in the popularity of annuities is the high commissions salespeople often receive—

resulting in aggressive sales approaches. Annuities are, and have always been, the highest commission financial product in the financial services industry. Unfortunately, these commissions compromise product recommendations with offerings that are not always in the investor's best interests. Annuity salespeople can receive commissions ranging from 5 to 10 percent of the invested amount, so a $100,000 annuity investment can earn them as much as $10,000. This financial incentive often encourages salespeople to promote annuities over more suitable investment options, leading to biased, substandard recommendations.

As a result of the high commissions paid by issuing insurance companies, investors typically face significant penalties if they need their money back after committing to an annuity. The issuer must control your money long enough to collect sufficient revenue from the underlying annual expenses of the annuity to make a profit. Consequently, surrender charges for annuities typically range from 5 to 15 percent of the amount invested, lasting anywhere from five to fifteen years.

The reality is that your needs can easily change over time, and these surrender charges severely limit access to your money. In addition, with internal expenses often exceeding 3 percent per year, annuities generate lower returns than other investment options. Experts like Warren Buffett and Dave Ramsey have long criticized annuities for their inferior performance and high fees.

The good news is that an increasing number of annuity products entering the market don't rely on high commissions or considerable surrender charges. If the guarantees of an annuity appeal to you, request the product's surrender charge schedule. The higher the charges and the longer they apply, the higher the commission the annuity will pay. Please avoid those products, as they are likely not in your best interest.

Caveat Emptor

Generally, annuities are not an ideal investment because they lack flexibility, deliver lower returns, and promote overselling with excessive commissions. Retirement-focused investors are lured by the guarantees offered by issuing insurance companies. Unfortunately, annuity issuers only offer the least possible guarantee to ensure their own profits.

Annuity sales always spike in times of fear, which is never an ideal time to make investment decisions that tie up money for a long time. Sadly, sales of these subpar investment vehicles continue to skyrocket. In the first half of 2023 alone, annuity sales hit $182.9 billion, a 28 percent increase compared to the same period in 2022.

If you own an annuity or have been approached to invest your money in one, please contact us at www.NelsonFinancialPlanning.com. We can clarify the fine print and explain how the product works. Caveat emptor – buyer beware when it comes to an annuity!

Questions & Notes

Chapter 11

Rates of Return and
the Economic Cycle

In the short term, stock market returns are always uncertain, but over time, investors experience positive results. Throughout its 100-year history, the stock market has been a reliable wealth-building tool for consistent and diversified investors. The stock market has prevailed despite numerous dramatic historical events because of the global economy's resilience. After each decline, markets have fully recovered and subsequently set new records. Let me say that again – *the stock market has always fully recovered over time from every one of its previous declines!*

As businesses continue to innovate and expand, the market reflects this growth and potential for value creation. Strong financial institutions and regulatory frameworks contribute to market stability, while diversified portfolios enable investors to withstand short-term volatility. Additionally, the market's ability to self-correct after crises displays its inherent strength and the importance of long-term investment strategies. Take a moment and think of all the dramatic headlines from the last century: two world wars, multiple conflicts, numerous acts of terrorism, political scandals, and more. Yet the stock market has persevered and continued its overall upward trend throughout history.

CAPITAL GROUP®

How long do recessions and bear markets last?

Recessions have been relatively small blips in economic history

- Over the last 70 years, the U.S. has been in an official recession less than 15% of all months.
- Moreover, the net longer term economic impact of most recessions has been relatively small.

Recessions are painful, but expansions have been powerful

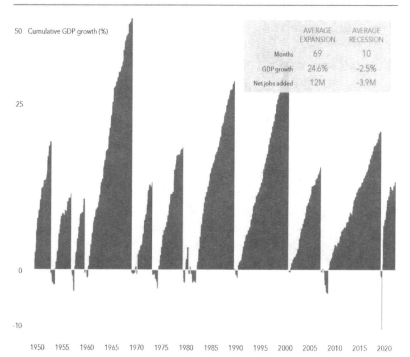

	AVERAGE EXPANSION	AVERAGE RECESSION
Months	69	10
GDP growth	24.6%	-2.5%
Net jobs added	12M	-3.9M

Sources: Capital Group, National Bureau of Economic Research (NBER), Refinitiv Datastream. Chart data is latest available as of 12/31/22 and shown on a logarithmic scale. The expansion that began in 2020 is still considered current as of 12/31/22, and is not included in the average expansion summary statistics. Since NBER announces recession start and end months, rather than exact dates, we have used month-end dates as a proxy for calculations of jobs added. Nearest quarter-end values used for GDP growth rates.

Investments are not FDIC-insured, nor are they deposits of or guaranteed by a bank or any other entity, so they may lose value.

To a considerable extent, the market ebbs and flows alongside the underlying economic cycle, which has periods of expansion and contraction. The stock market and the economic cycle are closely correlated, and economic factors often drive market performance. During economic growth, corporate earnings increase, and stock prices rise. Conversely, during economic downturns, earnings decline, investor pessimism peaks, and stock prices fall. Moreover, the stock market often anticipates and reacts to these economic shifts, further reflecting the intertwined relationship between the two.

As the graph on the left shows (courtesy of Capital Group), economic expansions last longer than contractions. Over the past seventy years, the average expansion lasted sixty-nine months, producing 24.6 percent of cumulative economic growth. The average recession, however, lasted just ten months with a 2.5 percent economic contraction.

Expansions prevail over the long term, contributing significantly to the sustained upward trajectory experienced by consistent investors. Despite this, people always remember the difficult years. Perhaps it is fundamental human nature, as the headlines in the table (courtesy of Putnam Investments) on the following page are forever etched in our minds! Who can forget the Great Financial Crisis of 2008, resulting in the collapse of Lehman Brothers and a 39.6 percent decline in the S&P 500? Unfortunately, most people don't recall the strength of the 48.8 percent recovery the following year.

In particular, the last two columns in the table on the following page (5 years later and 10 years later) highlight the market's resiliency, particularly after some of the worst periods ever for the stock market. A recovery produced a positive cumulative return in every instance over the subsequent five and ten year period following a dramatic market decline. While past performance is no guarantee of the future, the ability of the markets to recover throughout history is truly spectacular.

Markets recover from crises

A major crisis that causes the stock market to drop in value can be unsettling, but it does not spell the end for markets or investment strategies. History has shown that markets bounce back, and that staying invested through volatile episodes lets you benefit from a rebound.

Crisis and recovery: How the S&P 500 Index performed during and after historic events

Event	Event reaction dates	Percent of gain/ loss during event	S&P 500 percentage of gain/loss after last reaction date			
			1 month later	1 year later	5 years later	10 years later
Fall of France	5/9/40–6/21/40	−18.2%	3.1%	5.2%	15.9%	13.2%
Attack on Pearl Harbor	12/5/41–12/10/41	−6.9	4.5	16.0	18.1	17.1
Outbreak of Korean War	6/23/50–7/13/50	−11.1	9.5	42.0	27.6	18.4
U.S. invades Cambodia	4/29/70–5/26/70	−15.0	6.4	49.0	9.3	9.3
Nixon resigns	8/9/74–8/29/74	−13.4	−6.8	30.6	14.6	14.6
1987 stock market crash	10/16/87–10/19/87	−20.5	7.1	27.9	17.0	18.9
September 11 terrorist attacks	9/10/01–9/21/01	−11.6	11.3	−11.1	8.3	3.9
Collapse of Lehman Brothers	9/12/08–11/20/08	−39.6	18.3	48.8	21.5	15.8
U.S. debt downgrade by S&P	8/4/11–10/3/11	−8.1	14.9	35.0	17.0	17.1
U.K. Brexit referendum	6/23/16–6/27/16	−5.3	8.5	23.5	18.7	—
Covid-19 pandemic	2/19/20–3/23/20	−33.8	25.2	77.8	—	—
Mean gain/loss		**−16.7**	**9.3**	**31.3**	**16.8**	**14.3**
Median gain/loss		**−13.4**	**8.5**	**30.6**	**17.0**	**15.8**

The event reaction periods begin with the stock market close prior to the events.

Historical references do not assume that any prior market behavior will be duplicated. Past performance does not indicate future results.

There are risks associated with mutual fund investing including the possibility that share prices will decline. Since investment return and principal value will fluctuate, shares when redeemed may be worth more or less than their original cost. Performance of Putnam funds will differ.

The S&P 500® Index is an unmanaged index of common stock performance. You cannot invest directly in an index. Indexes are unmanaged and used as a broad measure of market performance.

Another graph on the following page (courtesy of Capital Group) further paints this picture from a pure market perspective. Over the same seventy-year period previously discussed from an economic perspective, market performance nearly mirrors the ebbs and flows of the economy.

Bull markets (periods when the market increases) last an average of sixty-seven months and produce an average total return of 265 percent. On the other hand, bear markets (periods when the markets decline) last only thirteen months, resulting in an average decline of 33 percent. This is an impressive history of recoveries that last much longer than market declines, thus producing superior results in the long term.

The average performance of stocks and bonds over time helps investors differentiate among investment choices. For the past one hundred years, inflation, as measured by the Consumer Price Index (CPI), has increased by nearly 3 percent per year, while the following has occurred:

- Short-term U.S. treasury bills grew slightly more than 3 percent

- Long-term U.S. government bonds earned 5 to 6 percent (depending on the bond maturity)

- Large company stocks, measured by the S&P 500, averaged nearly 10 percent

- Small company stocks averaged 11 to 12 percent (depending on the historical data utilized)

While past performance is no guarantee or predictor of the future, it is a useful tool to help investors decide among different types of investments. Of course, the better the returns, the greater the potential for volatility. The tradeoff between return and the potential for decline is the core balancing act in determining an investor's asset allocation—the focus of the next chapter.

Don't fear the bear

- Over the last 70 years, bear markets have been relatively short with limited losses when compared to the powerful bull markets that have followed.

- Aggressive market-timing moves during a downturn, such as shifting an entire portfolio into cash, can backfire.

Bear markets have been relatively short compared to bull markets

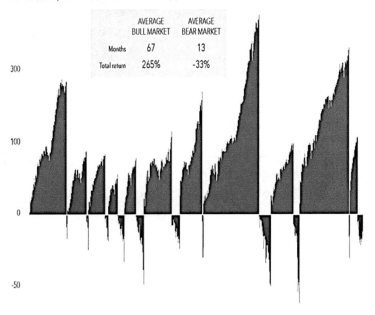

700 Cumulative price return for each bull and bear market (%)

	AVERAGE BULL MARKET	AVERAGE BEAR MARKET
Months	67	13
Total return	265%	-33%

Sources: Capital Group, RIMES, Standard & Poor's. As of 3/31/23. The bear market that began on 1/3/22 is considered current and is not included in the "average bear market" calculations. Bear markets are peak-to-trough price declines of 20% or more in the S&P 500. Bull markets are all other periods. Returns are in USD and shown on a logarithmic scale. Past results are not predictive of results in future periods.

Chapter 12

Asset Allocation

Asset allocation is the process of dividing your investments among different asset classes (like stocks, bonds, and cash) so all your proverbial eggs aren't in one basket. This strategy helps balance risk and reward by spreading investments across a range of assets that perform differently under varying market conditions.

Creating a Balanced Portfolio

Serving as a cornerstone of successful investing, asset allocation helps create a well-balanced portfolio that can withstand market fluctuations or volatility and still achieve long-term financial results.

A well-diversified portfolio typically includes a mix of stocks, bonds, and cash tailored to the investor's risk tolerance, financial goals, and investment horizon. While stocks are more suitable for investors seeking long-term growth and higher returns, bonds and cash are better for those seeking income and capital preservation.

Investors who combine these asset classes in various amounts get the best of both worlds: the gains of potential stock growth plus the stability of bonds and cash to mitigate volatility. This diversification helps manage risk and achieve consistent investment outcomes, contributing to a successful long-term financial strategy.

However, you must still be careful not to withdraw too much from your investment. Once retired, spending about 4 percent of your investment is considered sustainable. No amount of asset allocation will help if you spend too much from your accounts.

Weathering Market Volatility

Proper asset allocation minimizes the impact of market declines while capitalizing on overall investment trends. This approach helps protect your investments from excess market instability and economic uncertainties. For instance, cash offers liquidity and safety, bonds provide income and stability, and stocks offer growth potential but can fluctuate. Distributing your investments across these asset classes creates a well-rounded portfolio that balances risk and reward.

As we like to say, "Different things perform differently at different times." Owning different things (i.e., stocks, bonds, and cash) means you can always access part of your portfolio without worrying about its current value. We often refer to this as an "all-weather" portfolio. We don't know tomorrow's weather or headlines, but more stable assets within a diversified portfolio should be available at any time, regardless of the headlines.

Historical Perspective

The chart on the following page shows the historical performance of different stock and bond combinations since 1929. Unsurprisingly, a 100 percent stock portfolio achieved the best annualized performance over time at 10.3 percent but also had the single worst year, declining 43.1 percent. Similarly, a 100 percent bond portfolio had the lowest annualized performance at 5.3 percent but the smallest single-year decline of 8.1 percent.

Best, Worst, and Average Investment Returns

BY ASSET ALLOCATION

Below, we dive deeper into how asset allocations have impacted investment returns over 94 years.

Annual Returns 1926-2019

Worst Year		Allocation (Stocks / Bonds)	Average	Best Year
-8.1%		0% / 100%	5.3%	32.6%
-8.2%		10% / 90%	6.0%	31.2%
-10.1%		20% / 80%	6.6%	29.8%
-14.2%		30% / 70%	7.2%	28.4%
-18.4%		40% / 60%	7.8%	27.9%
-22.5%		50% / 50%	8.3%	32.3%
-26.6%		60% / 40%	8.8%	36.7%
-30.7%		70% / 30%	9.2%	41.1%
-34.9%		80% / 20%	9.6%	45.4%
-39.0%		90% / 10%	10.0%	49.8%
-43.1%		100% / 0%	10.3%	54.2%

Since **1926**, bonds have posted negative annual returns **15%** of the time.

% of Years With Negative Returns
28% Stocks | 23% 60/40 | 15% Bonds

A 60/40 portfolio had its worst year in **1931** as the U.S. economy faced a banking crisis and the money supply fell about **30%** between 1930-1933.

On average, the traditional 60/40 portfolio has returned **8.8%** annually.

While stocks are more volatile than bonds, they have averaged roughly **7%** in inflation-adjusted returns.

A $100 investment in 1926 in equities (with dividends reinvested) would have soared to over **$877K** by 2019.

MARKETS IN A MINUTE

Sources: Vanguard calculations, using data from Morningstar, Inc., Macrotrends, NYT, U.S. Federal Reserve, Robert Shiller

 VISUAL CAPITALIST RESEARCH + WRITING Dorothy Neufield | DESIGN VC

 /visualcapitalist @visualcap @visualcapitalist visualcapitalist.com

Stocks represented by the Standard & Poor's 90 Index from 1926 to March 3, 1957, the S&P 500 Index from March 4, 1957, through 1974, the Wilshire 5000 Index from 1975 through April 22, 2005, and the MSCI US Broad Market Index until 2019.

Bonds are represented by the S&P High Grade Corporate Index from 1926 through 1968, the Citigroup High Grade Index from 1969 through 1972, the Bloomberg Barclays U.S. Long Credit AA Index from 1973 through 1975, and the Bloomberg Barclays U.S. Aggregate Bond Index until 2019.

Asset allocation is all about striking the right balance between maximizing long-term growth and limiting the impact of short-term declines.

Age and Allocation

Your age is one of the most significant factors in crafting an appropriate asset allocation. As you approach retirement, your asset allocation should shift away from more volatile stocks toward more stable bonds and cash.

A young investor, for example, with a high-risk tolerance might allocate more of their portfolio to stocks, while a conservative investor nearing retirement may prioritize bonds and cash.

The pie charts below provide a general depiction of how asset allocation should change as you age. Remember that these formulistic asset allocations are no substitute for a tailored and thoughtful strategy that achieves your specific financial goals and objectives.

Asset Allocation by Age

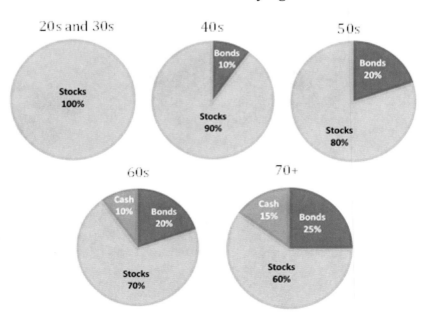

Avoid the Scatter

At Nelson Financial Planning, selecting the proper asset allocation for investors is vitally important. Moreover, a targeted and refined approach creates more growth potential with less risk than the haphazard scatter method broadly favored by the financial services industry.

This scattered approach to allocation attempts to achieve balance with an extensive array of assets, resulting in investors owning all sizes of companies in all parts of the world.

The reality is that small companies experience more volatility than large ones, just as companies from emerging economies like Bangladesh have greater risk than ones in the United States.

As a result of owning these more aggressive asset categories, investors must then balance their overall portfolio risk by investing a larger portion more conservatively. This is a significant limitation of the scattered allocation approach because it unnecessarily increases the bond and cash portions of one's portfolio just to offset more aggressive stock holdings.

We believe your asset allocation should be specifically tailored, not partially designed simply to offset the risk of specific holdings. If your portfolio does not hold small or emerging market companies to begin with, it will have less risk than a portfolio that does. Unlike the typical scattered approach, our tailored approach of owning more large companies from developed markets provides you the freedom to hold a greater proportion of stocks in your portfolio. Owning more stocks over time then provides clients the opportunity to achieve better results while maintaining the same overall risk profile.

Questions & Notes

Chapter 13

The Average Person's DIY Results

Have you ever bought a house from someone who fancied themselves as a bit of a do-it-yourselfer? They believe they can do anything around the house with a simple trip to Home Depot and a few YouTube videos. Sure, they may save some money by not hiring a professional. But the time, effort, and rework necessary to bring their DIY attempt up to acceptable standards always add up to a pretty penny—often more than hiring a professional in the first place.

The same analogy applies to people who follow the do-it-yourself approach with their financial and retirement decisions using online tools or 1-800 numbers. Unfortunately, human emotions (discussed thoroughly in Chapter 1) can lead to faulty decisions at the worst possible time. Studies show that those online tools are nothing more than general guidelines applicable to only 5 percent of the population. As for the 1–800 number call centers, it is doubtful that the person on the other end of the line has much experience—assuming it is a live person and not some artificial intelligence-based system.

Those approaches certainly provide cheaper alternatives for managing your money, but personally tailored, fiduciary-based guidance can help you stay on track throughout life's ups and downs more effectively.

Unfortunately, the financial services industry does not have a great track record for always providing advice in the customer's best interest. It is common to see professional investment advisory or management services costing more than 1 percent per year. It's imperative to carefully research anyone you plan to use for financial guidance and ensure you fully understand all their service costs.

Just as Miguel Cabrera, the Major League Baseball player with over three thousand hits, has a hitting coach, we believe all investors should have a financial coach. The game of life tends to throw curveballs, causing us to react and make a foul play. An experienced coach can help you navigate life's decisions better than going alone. After all, human emotions can lead to faulty decisions at the worst possible time.

Anyone assisting with your finances should be a fiduciary with many years of experience. While financial advisors and planners generally offer a wide variety of services, only fiduciaries are legally obligated to act in their clients' best interests. Any advisor should focus on guiding your decisions, not dictating them—after all, it is your money, not theirs! That's why at Nelson Financial Planning, all the members of our financial planning team are Certified Financial Fiduciaries® with an average of more than twenty years of experience.

We have never required clients to meet any minimum account thresholds because we have always focused first on helping people. It saddens us to hear advertisements for other firms requiring minimum investments of $500,000 or $1 million. How can a firm claim its goal is to help people on their financial journey if they only want to help those who have already accumulated sizable wealth on their own?

Mistakes made using the DIY approach can significantly damage any long-term financial progress. The average investor stymies their investment results in three distinct (and much studied) ways, beyond overpaying for poor advisory services or relying on the internet and 1-800 numbers.

Average Investor vs. Market

The first mistake is that the average investor typically underperforms the stock market due to various behavioral biases and suboptimal investment strategies. Factors such as emotional decision-making, lack of diversification, poor market timing, and high trading costs contribute to this underperformance. Chapter 1 of this book discusses how emotions impact human behavior and cause unintended bias. In contrast, the stock market benefits from diversification across industry sectors and participation in long-term economic growth cycles, as discussed in Chapter 11. Investors must ignore the media to improve their financial outcomes, stay consistent, and focus on achieving long-term results. Otherwise, they may retire with much less money than they could have.

As the graph on the following page shows (courtesy of MFS Investments), the average investor missed out on about 30 percent of the market's annualized return over the past thirty years. That's a huge difference! Considering the power of compound growth, you could wind up retiring with less than half of what you should have!

Missing the Best Days

The second mistake is timing. History tells us that many of the market's very best days occur near the market's worst days. This volatility is gut-wrenching, as nobody likes to see their account balances dramatically

The Average Investor Underperformed[1]

When investors tried to protect their portfolios by moving in and out of the market, they often limited gains and increased losses instead

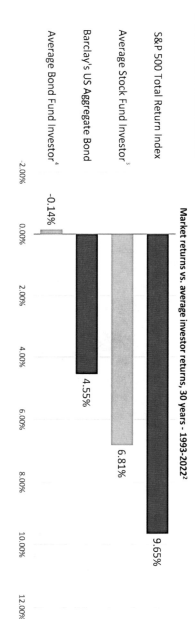

Market returns vs. average investor returns, 30 years - 1993-2022[2]

S&P 500 Total Return Index	9.65%
Average Stock Fund Investor[3]	6.81%
Barclay's US Aggregate Bond	4.55%
Average Bond Fund Investor[4]	-0.14%

Axis: -2.00% 0.00% 2.00% 4.00% 6.00% 8.00% 10.00% 12.00%

Source: Dalbar, 2023 QAIB Report, as of December 31, 2022.

This example is for illustrative purposes only and are not intended to represent the future performance of any MFS™ product. Although the data is gathered from sources believed to be reliable, MFS cannot guarantee the accuracy and/or completeness of the information.

1 The Average Investor refers to the universe of all mutual funds investors whose actions and financial results are restated to represent a single investor. This approach allows the entire universe of mutual funds investors to be used as the statistical sample, ensuring ultimate reliability.

2 Average investor return performance. Methodology: QAIB calculates investor returns as the change in assets, after excluding sales, redemptions, and exchanges. This method of calculation captures investor returns realized and unrealized capital gains, dividends, interest, trading costs, sales charges, fees, expenses and any other costs. After calculating investor returns in dollar terms, two percentages are calculated: total investor rate for the period and annualized investor return rate. Total return rate is determined by calculating the investor return dollars as a percentage of the net assets, sales, redemptions and exchanges for the period. Annualized return rate is calculated as the uniform rate that can be compounded annually for the period under consideration to produce the investor return dollars.

3 The Average Equity Fund Investor comprises a universe of both domestic and world equity mutual funds. It includes growth, sector, alternative strategy, value, blend emerging markets, global equity, international equity and regional equity.

4 The Average Fixed Income Investor is comprised of a universe of fixed income mutual funds, which includes investment- grade, high-yield, government, municipal, multisector, and global bond funds. It does not include money market funds.

The S&P 500 Total Return Index measures the broad US stock market. **Bloomberg Barclays U.S. Aggregate Bond Index** measures the U.S. bond market.

Past performance is no guarantee of future results. Keep in mind that all investments carry a certain amount of risk, including the possible loss of the principal amount invested.

decrease. Unfortunately, the average person reacts to those significant down days by shifting their portfolio around at the worst possible time. Missing just a few of the best days in the stock market can significantly impact investment returns, which is why the "Consistency" concept in Chapter 2 is so important.

The chart on the following page (courtesy again of MFS Investments) demonstrates how dramatically this can impact your long-term results. Over a span of twenty years, missing just the ten best days in the S&P 500 resulted in a 50 percent reduction in returns. That's right—a 50 percent reduction for missing just ten days out of the more than five thousand market trading days within twenty years. The difference in the amount of money that could have been in your retirement account is staggering. Since it's difficult to time the market effectively, staying invested long-term is critical to achieving your investment goals. Bottom line: stick to your investment plan (assuming you carefully read the prior chapter and your asset allocation is where it needs to be!).

At Nelson Financial Planning, we believe investors should have an ongoing perspective about current headlines without letting the daily news drive investment decisions. The media does a great job elaborating on worst-case scenarios, causing investors to make emotional, reactive decisions about their financial plans. However, a financial plan is specifically designed to accomplish its goals over an extended period—not a matter of days. Regular, proactive communication is an ideal primary method to help investors maintain perspective. Educational information empowers people to better navigate life's ups and downs.

Why Should I Stick to the Plan?

When markets get a little volatile, people tend to let emotions take over, and they make irrational decisions with regard to their portfolios. What's more, news headlines often lead to short-term investment decisions that are costly and destructive. That's why it's important for you to use a disciplined approach based on your risk profile.

If you missed the best days of the market

Growth of $10,000 in the S&P 500 vs. average investor, 30 years ending December 31, 2022.

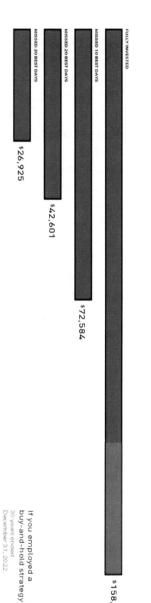

FULLY INVESTED — $158,434

MISSED 10 BEST DAYS — $72,584

MISSED 20 BEST DAYS — $42,601

MISSED 30 BEST DAYS — $26,925

If you employed a buy-and-hold strategy
30 years ended December 31, 2022.

S&P 500 — 9.65%

AVERAGE INVESTOR RETURN — 6.81%

Past performance is no guarantee of future results.

The **S&P 500 Index** measures the broad U.S. stock market. Index performance does not include any investment-related fees or expenses. It is not possible to invest directly in an index.

Keep in mind that all investments, including mutual funds, carry a certain amount of risk, including the possible loss of the principal amount invested.

Source: "DALBAR Quantitative Analysis of Investor Behavior 2023" Advisor Edition. Data is as of 12/31/22. Methodology: DALBAR's Quantitative Analysis of Investor Behavior (QAIB) uses data from the Investment Company Institute (ICI), S&P 500, Barclays Capital Index Products and proprietary sources to compare mutual fund investor returns to an appropriate set of benchmarks. Covering the period from QAIB's inception (January 1, 1984) to December 31, 2022, the study utilizes mutual fund sales, redemptions and exchanges each month as the measure of investor behavior. These behaviors reflect the "average investor." Based on the behavior, the analysis calculates the "average investor return" for various periods. These results are then compared to the returns of respective indices.

The Cost of Procrastination

Sometimes, we all put off things until later, when we know we should do them now. Unfortunately, procrastinating now has costly consequences for future savings. Waiting is the third big mistake people often make with their investments.

While waiting for the perfect time to invest is tempting, trying to time any investment into the market is nearly impossible. Remember the "Time In, Not Timing" concept from Chapter 2? Historically, the stock market produces positive returns over the long term, but in the short term, it is much more volatile. Plus, waiting to invest shortens your overall investing time period, which can require you to increase your savings later on or, worse, adopt a more aggressive approach to catch up.

With investing, starting early makes a significant difference in your end results. The example on the following page compares two investors.

- **Investor A** starts saving $250 monthly at age twenty-two, but only for the first ten years.

- **Investor B** waits ten years and then, at age thirty-two, starts saving the same $250 monthly and continues saving this amount through age sixty-five—for a total of thirty-four years.

The bottom line results over time are shocking! Assuming a 10 percent return for both investors, at age sixty-five, Investor A accumulates $1,343,641 while Investor B only accrues $810,073. What's worse, Investor B contributed three times the amount of money over a much longer period than Investor A but still had nearly 40 percent less in his account. Why did Investor A come out so far ahead? Investor A didn't procrastinate and started saving just ten years earlier than Investor B. The power of time and compounding truly produces impressive results.

Procrastination Costs

Compare these two investors (assuming a 10% annual rate of return)

Investor A: Starts at age 22, invests $3,000 annually for only 10 years
Investor B: Starts at age 32, invests $3,000 annually for 34 years (through age 65)

Age	Invest	Accumulation	Age	Invest	Accumulation
22	$3,000	$3,300	22	0	0
23	$3,000	$6,930	23	0	0
24	$3,000	$10,923	24	0	0
25	$3,000	$15,315	25	0	0
26	$3,000	$20,147	26	0	0
27	$3,000	$25,462	27	0	0
28	$3,000	$31,308	28	0	0
29	$3,000	$37,738	29	0	0
30	$3,000	$44,812	30	0	0
31	$3,000	$52,594	31	0	0
32	0	$57,853	32	$3,000	$3,300
33	0	$63,638	33	$3,000	$6,930
34	0	$70,002	34	$3,000	$10,923
35	0	$77,002	35	$3,000	$15,315
36	0	$84,702	36	$3,000	$20,147
37	0	$93,173	37	$3,000	$25,462
38	0	$102,490	38	$3,000	$31,308
39	0	$112,739	39	$3,000	$37,738
40	0	$124,013	40	$3,000	$44,812
41	0	$136,414	41	$3,000	$52,594
42	0	$150,055	42	$3,000	$61,152
43	0	$165,061	43	$3,000	$70,568
44	0	$181,567	44	$3,000	$80,924
45	0	$199,724	45	$3,000	$92,317
46	0	$219,696	46	$3,000	$104,849
47	0	$241,666	47	$3,000	$118,634
48	0	$265,832	48	$3,000	$133,797
49	0	$292,416	49	$3,000	$150,477
50	0	$321,657	50	$3,000	$168,825
51	0	$353,823	51	$3,000	$189,007
52	0	$389,205	52	$3,000	$211,208
53	0	$428,126	53	$3,000	$235,629
54	0	$470,938	54	$3,000	$262,491
55	0	$518,031	55	$3,000	$292,041
56	0	$569,835	56	$3,000	$324,545
57	0	$626,819	57	$3,000	$360,299
58	0	$689,500	58	$3,000	$399,629
59	0	$758,451	59	$3,000	$442,892
60	0	$834,296	60	$3,000	$490,482
61	0	$917,725	61	$3,000	$542,830
62	0	$1,009,498	62	$3,000	$600,412
63	0	$1,110,447	63	$3,000	$663,754
64	0	$1,221,480	64	$3,000	$733,430
65	0	**$1,343,641**	65	$3,000	**$810,073**
Total	**$30,000**		**Total**	**$102,000**	
	Investor A			**Investor B**	

Past performance is no guarantee of future results. Figures shown are for illustration purposes and do not represent a specific outcome.

A Solution to Procrastination

In Chapter 2, we discussed the importance of paying yourself first, which is also a very effective tactic for overcoming procrastination. Market volatility is a normal part of investing, but one of the best ways to mitigate short-term market swings is to invest regularly. This concept, known as dollar-cost averaging, has a proven track record of generating positive results over time while smoothing out the ups and downs of the market.

Here is how to make this concept work for you. Commit to investing a fixed amount of money at regular intervals over time. For example, set up an automatic withdrawal from your checking account to subtract $250 on the first of each month to go directly into your investment account. Alternatively, you could allocate 10 percent of every paycheck directly into an employer-provided retirement plan.

These habits significantly help reduce the risk of investing during a market high by spreading your investments over time. Your fixed contribution will buy less of your selected investment when the market is up. However, when the market is down, those same dollars buy more and help balance out the impact of short-term market volatility on your invested dollars. Dollar-cost averaging is simple to do and is a great way to overcome procrastination and achieve investment results over time.

Questions & Notes

Chapter 14

Life's Big Purchases

With such a significant amount of money involved, buying a home is usually the single largest financial transaction of one's entire life. You'll likely feel the ramifications of any home-buying decision for years to come. If you make a mistake, the cost of changing things can be significant.

However, homeownership is beneficial to one's overall financial picture and personal life. Beyond providing a sense of stability and community, real estate typically appreciates over time, allowing you to build personal wealth. More importantly, owning a home offers the freedom to personalize and modify your living space according to your tastes, bringing a sense of pride and accomplishment.

The entire homebuying process comes with many decisions, but taking time to understand the details involved in buying a home helps you plan ahead and avoid any ramifications or regrets.

When to Buy?

One question people often face is choosing the right time to purchase a home. That decision is unique to each person, but we recommend considering the following factors when making this commitment:

- **Financial Stability:** Before buying a house, you should have a stable income, a healthy credit score, and enough savings for a down payment, typically 20 percent of the home's price. These savings should not include the money in your emergency fund, which is to cover unexpected expenses (discussed in Chapter 4).

- **Market Options:** Take the time to research current housing market trends in your desired area and view a variety of houses to assess what works best for your personal needs.

- **Personal Goals:** Review your personal long-term plans and lifestyle needs before committing to buying a house. If you plan to live in an area for at least five to seven years or have a growing family, buying a home may be a wise investment. However, renting might be more suitable if you anticipate frequent moves or job changes.

- **Affordability:** Analyze the cost of owning a home, including mortgage payments, property taxes, insurance, and maintenance. Ensure these expenses fit comfortably within your budget without compromising your financial goals or quality of life. Getting pre-qualified for a potential mortgage helps clarify an appropriate price range for your financial situation before getting too excited about a particular neighborhood or house.

- **Preparedness for Homeownership:** Owning a home comes with responsibilities, such as maintenance, repairs, and lawn care. Ensure you are ready to take on these tasks and commit to the long-term responsibilities of homeownership from both a time and financial perspective.

Borrowing Money for a Home Purchase

When buying a home, most people borrow money in the form of a mortgage loan to help with the purchase. A mortgage is typically owed to a bank or other lending institution, secured by the home or real estate purchased using the proceeds of the mortgage. Because a mortgage is a secured loan, failing to pay the loan according to its terms can result in the financial institution foreclosing on the home or acquiring it to satisfy the outstanding amount of the loan. Still, using a mortgage to buy a home is a sound financial decision for many reasons.

- **Credit**: It is an excellent use of credit to improve your overall financial picture since paying your mortgage regularly over time helps boost your credit score.

- **Leverage**: It allows you to use leverage, a financial concept of using less cash up front, to purchase a home rather than financing the entire purchase price from your savings.

- **Affordability**: Spreading out the cost of a home over an extended period through monthly payments helps you afford to purchase a home.

- **Appreciation**: Real estate generally appreciates over time, so owning a home helps improve your overall net worth.

What's in a Mortgage Payment?

There are five different components of a mortgage payment; understanding each is essential to comprehending how mortgages work and where your money goes.

Principal

This is the portion of your mortgage payment that directly pays down the outstanding amount of the mortgage. If you submit any additional amount above your regular mortgage payment, you can reduce the time it takes to pay off the loan's outstanding balance. Paying one extra mortgage payment per year at the start of your mortgage will shorten the term of a thirty-year mortgage by nearly five years. This is a great way to achieve the key recommended goal of fully paying off your mortgage before retirement.

Interest

This is the finance cost (or interest rate) associated with your mortgage. In the first several years of a mortgage, more of your payment will be allocated towards interest. Over time, as you make more payments, the portion dedicated to the principal gradually increases, and the interest portion decreases. The amount you pay as interest is tax deductible when you itemize your deductions, as discussed in more detail in Chapter 16.

Taxes

This part has nothing to do with your mortgage itself. Instead, it ensures your annual real estate taxes are paid by adding them to your monthly mortgage payment, which is then held in an escrow account. This protects the lender's interest in your home as the highest priority in a foreclosure. This escrow approach forces you to budget for your real estate taxes as part of your mortgage payment and is required for some mortgages. Personally, I have never escrowed my taxes as part of my mortgage payment. I prefer budgeting money each month and paying my taxes directly, rather than relying on the bank to control this. If you have the option to avoid escrowing this cost, you should do so, but only if you budget for your taxes accordingly.

Insurance

This is another part of your payment that doesn't directly impact your underlying mortgage. Instead, it is another escrow account involving your homeowner's insurance. In essence, the lender collects your insurance premium on your behalf each month and then remits it every year to your insurance company. Some mortgages require escrowed insurance, but if you can opt out, we suggest budgeting for this cost on your own.

Private Mortgage Insurance (PMI)

This is the one component of a mortgage payment you should avoid at all costs. PMI usually applies when the downpayment for your home purchase is less than 20 percent of the purchase price. On a $300,000 mortgage, PMI typically increases your mortgage payment by an extra $250 each month. This insurance isn't even designed to help you. It simply protects the bank's ability to make an insurance claim for any financial shortfall if it must foreclose on the home and its value is less than the amount owed on the mortgage. Avoid this extra cost on your mortgage payment, as it does not benefit you and adds up considerably over time!

Which Mortgage is the Right One?

So, now you are ready to purchase a house! But what mortgage should you use? Selecting the right mortgage involves analyzing multiple factors, with the most relevant considerations discussed below.

Interest Rate

This is the most crucial factor to review when deciding between mortgages. The interest rate determines the total cost you will pay for borrowing money, so the lower the rate, the lower the loan cost over time. While this mortgage interest is tax deductible, most people don't get that tax benefit because of the higher standard deduction (discussed more in Chapter 16). Your interest rate will reflect the current interest rate environment, so you'll want to monitor the market before you get ready to buy a house. Typically, the yield on the long-term Treasury bond drives mortgage rate pricing (discussed in Chapter 8).

The rate environment will be a significant factor in deciding whether to obtain a fixed or variable-rate mortgage. A fixed-rate mortgage includes an interest rate that is fixed for the entire mortgage term. At the same time, a variable-rate mortgage (also known as an adjustable-rate mortgage or ARM) will set the interest rate for an initial period, usually between three and five years. After that initial period, the ARM rate will fluctuate based on the new prevailing interest rates. ARMs are a worthwhile option in higher interest rate environments because the interest rate for the initial period is typically below prevailing rates. They are also beneficial if you only plan to own the property for a short time. If you expect interest rates to decline or the property to appreciate in value, then you can refinance or trade in your existing mortgage for a new one at updated rates. However, if interest rates continue to increase or you fail to qualify for refinancing, an ARM could create higher costs over time.

As a result of historically low mortgage rates throughout the past decade, most people today have fixed-rate mortgages. With increasing interest rates, ARMs could become a more popular option for new homebuyers. In the late 90s, when interest rates spiked, I used an ARM to purchase my first home in Orlando. A few years later, after the house had appreciated and interest rates declined, I refinanced into a lower-rate mortgage.

Term

The length, or term, of your mortgage directly impacts the amount of your monthly payment and the length of time until it is fully paid off (assuming regular, consistent payments). A longer term generally requires a lower monthly payment because the payback period is extended, but the total interest cost also increases. At the same time, a shorter-term mortgage has a lower interest rate because the quicker payback period lowers the bank's risk of a homeowner defaulting on their loan.

Based on interest rates in mid-2023, a typical 30-year mortgage has a rate of 6.75 percent. Interestingly, this rate is virtually identical to mortgage rates from twenty-five years ago—the more things change, the more they stay the same! For each $100,000 borrowed, the monthly payment is $648.50. At the same time, a fifteen-year mortgage has a slightly lower rate of 6.37 percent, resulting in a monthly payment of $864.25 on a $100,000 mortgage. In this case, the monthly payment on the fifteen-year mortgage is 33 percent more than the comparable thirty-year mortgage. This difference might very well determine what you can afford. Unfortunately, with the extended period of a thirty-year mortgage, the total interest cost is $133,493.82, while the interest cost for the fifteen-year mortgage is only $55,565.04. That's a pretty significant cost difference!

If you start with a thirty-year mortgage because it fits your current budget, we recommend making extra payments often or refinancing to a shorter-term mortgage when interest rates decline. Doing this will help pay off your mortgage sooner and improve your retirement picture!

Loan-to-Value Amount

This ratio is calculated by dividing your loan amount by the property's value, and ideally, it should be less than 80 percent to avoid the PMI discussed earlier. A larger downpayment lowers this ratio and reduces your loan amount. This is why we recommend having a portion of your savings dedicated to a home downpayment fund to avoid the extra cost of PMI and reduce the amount you must borrow.

Closing Costs

The costs associated with obtaining a mortgage typically equal about 2 percent of the borrowed amount and include fees for preparing loan paperwork and securing the bank's interest in the property. They can be paid upfront or rolled into the total amount financed. Closing costs are one aspect of a loan where shopping around can pay off, as these costs vary widely among lenders.

Much of your decision about which mortgage is right for you depends on the current interest rate environment. If interest rates are high, you may want a mortgage with a longer term or even an adjustable rate feature. If interest rates are low, getting a mortgage with a shorter term or fixed rate makes more sense. When interest rates dropped to below 3 percent in 2021, many homeowners locked in this low rate on a fixed basis and shaved years of payments off their mortgages.

Home Equity Lines

A home equity line of credit (HELOC) is a type of loan allowing homeowners to borrow against the appreciation in their home. A HELOC operates as a revolving line of credit you can draw from as needed, providing flexibility to use the funds for various purposes like home improvements, debt consolidation, or unexpected expenses. In addition, since these funds represent your home's equity, there are no tax implications for accessing these monies.

Because this is a secured loan with your home as collateral, it typically has lower interest rates than other loans, such as personal loans or credit cards. While the interest paid can be tax-deductible, the interest rate is usually not fixed, so any rate increase will also cause the payment to increase. The monthly payment for this loan is also a function of the amount borrowed—the more you borrow from the line, the higher the payment. Like any other type of loan, you will undergo an approval process with a lender, and this additional debt can negatively impact your credit.

A home equity line represents a very flexible and cost-effective option for obtaining access to money, especially if the alternative is a high-interest credit card or a fully taxable retirement account. However, a HELOC is debt, and utilizing debt should always be done responsibly. Don't use this type of loan to finance your summer vacation!

Purchasing a Car

Purchasing a vehicle is often the second largest financial transaction people make in their lives. Like buying a house, the first step is reviewing your budget to calculate what you can afford. Don't forget ongoing costs like insurance, fuel, and maintenance. It is also essential to consider your personal needs, such as passenger capacity, cargo space, or fuel efficiency. Take your time and research things like reliability, safety, typical resale value, and, of course, the all-important test drive.

The biggest financial issue with cars is that far too many people treat them as status symbols. They view owning a particular car as a reflection of their wealth and success, wanting others to see them in the latest, greatest, and coolest vehicle. Car prices range widely—from the latest, fully loaded Mercedes-Benz S-Class at nearly $150,000 to a reliable and affordable Toyota Corolla for less than $25,000. If your tastes exceed your budget, you can easily undermine your overall financial stability. After all, a car should be considered a method of transportation and not a means to impress your friends.

Another concern with car buying is the practice of trading in for a new one every few years. Unlike real estate or other assets, cars depreciate quickly—on average, 20 percent the first year and 15 percent each year for the next three years. So, your "new" car will only be worth 35 percent of its original price in four years.

Conversely, owning a car for many years can result in paying it off entirely. Without that monthly car payment, you'll have extra money for other goals. You also save money on insurance costs, as older cars cost less to insure than newer cars. I drive a nine-year-old fully paid-off Ford Expedition that has over 100,000 miles. It has a few dents and scratches and doesn't have all the latest technology, but it gets me where I need to go pretty cost-effectively.

Cash, Finance, or Lease?

There are three distinct payment methods for acquiring a car, each with advantages and disadvantages.

- **Cash:** Purchasing with cash is a great way to avoid the extra expense in your budget, but it does reduce your available savings. That's why it helps to establish a car fund as part of your budget to earmark money specifically for a future car purchase or at least a significant down payment.

- **Financing**: This allows you to spread out the expense over time but adds interest rate costs. Car financing rates can be much higher than for homes, so you must be careful about overpaying for a car loan. As with anything, shop around and compare interest rates, costs, and terms for any car loan.

- **Leasing**: While this sometimes affords a lower monthly payment than financing, it is essentially just renting a car. As with renting a house, you have no actual ownership of the vehicle when you lease it. In addition, lease agreements typically have numerous restrictive provisions that create additional expenses at the end of the lease term.

Insurance

The total cost of insurance coverage for your health, home, and auto typically represents the third most significant financial expense people regularly incur. In its basic form, insurance is a contract between an individual (the policyholder) and an insurance company designed to protect against potential risks and losses. In exchange for regular premium payments, the insurance company agrees to compensate the policyholder for covered losses or damages as specified in the insurance policy. Insurance coverage can include a range of categories, such as:

- Property (e.g., home or car insurance)
- Health Insurance
- Life Insurance
- Business Insurance
- Liability / Umbrella Insurance

How Insurance Works

An insurance policy, which is a legal document that defines the rights and obligations of both the policyholder and insurance company, outlines the policy's specific terms and coverage details. The terms and conditions of any health, car, or homeowner policy can vary widely.

When an insured event occurs, such as an accident, death, theft, illness, or damage, the policyholder can file a claim with the insurance company. If the claim is covered under the policy, the insurance company will provide financial compensation or other benefits to help mitigate the losses incurred by the policyholder. The amount paid is subject to the limits and conditions specified in the policy.

Insurance plays a crucial role in your financial picture because it helps manage and transfer risk, provides financial protection, and affords peace of mind in the face of unexpected and costly events. When it comes to insurance, we recommend you engage fully with your insurance provider to make the best possible decision with the most appropriate balance of coverage and cost.

Umbrella Policies

We generally recommend an umbrella policy to provide additional liability protection beyond the limits of your car or home insurance policies. This type of insurance protects you from significant financial losses that may result from a lawsuit or liability claim against you. As your net worth grows, this additional umbrella insurance becomes more important to protect your assets.

Life Insurance

Our other general insurance recommendation involves life insurance. There are two types of life insurance: whole and term. The choice between whole and term life insurance depends on individual circumstances, financial goals, and preferences. Term life insurance is often suitable for those seeking temporary coverage at an affordable price. In contrast, whole life insurance may be ideal for individuals seeking lifelong coverage and potential cash value accumulation.

Term life insurance covers a specified term or period, such as ten, twenty, or thirty years. The policy premium is fixed during the coverage period and will not change. If the policyholder passes away during the term, a death benefit is paid to the beneficiaries. In this regard, a term policy offers greater flexibility because it can be tailored to specific needs when they are most important, such as covering a mortgage or providing for dependents until they reach adulthood. Since it only includes coverage for a specific period, term life insurance has much lower premiums than whole life insurance.

In contrast, whole life insurance is permanent coverage that can accumulate cash value and last the insured's entire life as long as premiums are paid annually. Because the underlying cost of insuring your life increases as you age, your annual whole-life policy premiums often increase over time.

Using term life insurance encourages disciplined savings practices. Instead of relying on the cash value component of a whole-life policy, you can invest the difference in cost between term and whole-life premiums in other investments. These alternatives can have better returns over time, offer more direct control, and provide greater flexibility than an insurance policy. The reality is that insurance should be used for insurance purposes, not investment purposes.

We generally prefer term over whole policies because they are much more cost-effective and provide flexibility by covering specific periods that coincide with the most significant periods of need. This is the type of policy I purchased when my three sons were young. We hadn't saved much money at that stage in our lives, and I could get significant coverage without paying a hefty premium. Over time, my assets grew, and my children became more independent as they got older, so the need for the policy diminished, and it lapsed when the term ended.

Questions & Notes

Chapter 15

College Planning

Obtaining a college education in America has become staggeringly expensive, with the average cost of a four-year degree surpassing $100,000 for public schools and nearing $225,000 at private universities.

Attending college is still incredibly valuable for learning new skills and earning a degree that many professions and industries now consider a minimum qualification. Additionally, the U.S. Bureau of Labor Statistics reports that bachelor's degree holders make about 40 percent more than those with just a high school diploma.

However, today's rising college education costs require a more rigorous cost-benefit analysis to calculate the value of attending a particular college. Additionally, many vocations that don't require college degrees now provide much higher wages and benefits and are experiencing significant staffing shortages. The earning potential within the skilled trade professions is surprisingly high.

If you choose to go to college, be smart about your decision. Research the expected salaries relative to your selected field of study so you don't end up with excessive student loan debt that is extremely difficult to pay off, given your chosen career.

Planning Ahead

Preparing for college or graduate school as early as possible is crucial to reducing future financial stress. As with any major purchase, it's essential to create a realistic budget that includes the full range of education-related expenses, including tuition, textbooks, housing, food, and transportation. Fortunately, there are various ways to significantly reduce the total cost of a college degree.

- Apply for scholarships and grants.

- Inquire about opportunities through your school's financial aid office.

- Leverage community colleges to complete prerequisite courses at a lower cost.

- Obtain college credits while in high school through dual enrollment programs or AP classes.

Unfortunately, most people do not adequately plan ahead for all these costs and must borrow money to attend school, which is how higher education costs quickly spiral out of control. Since loans start accruing interest immediately, the total owed at graduation is typically 35 percent higher than what was initially borrowed. In addition, interest rates on educational loans are costly, as shown below in the rates for the 2023-2024 academic year:

- Federal student loan interest rates are 4.99 percent for undergraduates and 6.54 percent for graduate students.

- Parent-based loan rates are 7.54 percent.

- Private student loan interest rates are even higher, typically 10 to 12 percent.

It is no wonder that the average student loan debt at graduation is nearly $30,000 for a public university and almost $55,000 for those who went to a private college. To reduce the long-term impact of this debt on your finances, you must plan as early as possible. Remember, the power of time and compounding works just as well with saving for college or graduate school!

The four primary savings vehicles available to help with educational costs are described in detail in this chapter. Choosing the right savings option for your child's education depends on several factors, including your financial goals, risk tolerance, and the type of education you anticipate for your child. Each has advantages and disadvantages, so understanding the differences will help you make an informed decision for the future.

Uniform Transfers to Minors Act

A Uniform Transfers to Minors Act (UTMA) account is a custodial account established for minors to hold assets, such as cash, stocks, bonds, or mutual funds until they reach the age of legal majority (typically 18). The account is managed by a custodian, typically a parent or guardian, who is responsible for making investment decisions on behalf of the minor. A UTMA account is the legal property of the child, and once established, the account ownership cannot change.

UTMA accounts provide a direct, simple way to transfer assets to a minor without needing a trust. UTMAs do not offer tax savings for educational purposes but can be taxed at the child's income tax rate, which is usually lower than the parents' rate. The account works like any other non-retirement account, providing broad flexibility with assets available for any purpose.

However, once the minor reaches the legal age of majority, they gain complete control over the account and can use the funds for any purpose whatsoever.

This can create some negative consequences. Years ago, there was a court case in New Jersey where, upon becoming an adult, the child hired an attorney to gain control over the assets in his UTMA account. The child/adult won the case and spent that money traveling through Europe rather than attending college. This case represented a perfect storm of dysfunctional family dynamics and unintended consequences!

Prepaid College Plans

A prepaid college plan allows families to prepay future college costs at today's rates, effectively locking in current prices and protecting against future inflation. The internal growth of these plans is designed to reflect the increase in college costs over time. Typically sponsored by state governments, these plans are designed for use at in-state public colleges and universities without tax implications on their benefits when used for educational expenses. Some plans even offer a la carte pricing to select coverage for various costs, including tuition or room and board. Participating in a prepaid tuition plan secures a future college education at a known, fixed price on a risk-free basis because the plan automatically covers costs exceeding the original projections.

Any adult can set up a prepaid plan for a named beneficiary, but it must be used within ten years of the projected college enrollment date of the designated beneficiary. However, the intended beneficiary can change to another family member. If your child does not attend college, the plan typically refunds your original payment amount without interest or adjustments for inflation. Additionally, if your child receives a scholarship or attends an out-of-state school, you can receive a refund equivalent to the value the plan would have paid otherwise.

These plans clearly favor in-state public schools but do not guarantee acceptance at a particular college or university and require state residency to enroll.

Prepaid college tuition plans are primarily suitable for families who are confident their child will attend an in-state public college or university. Unfortunately, we've seen many clients over the years surprised and disappointed when their children decided to attend out-of-state schools despite being fully indoctrinated as youngsters here in Central Florida with Gator, Knight, or Seminole culture.

Accurately predicting the future college plans of your children is tricky, which is why we don't typically recommend prepaid college accounts.

Educational IRA

An Educational IRA, also known as a Coverdell Education Savings Account (ESA), is a tax-advantaged investment account established, owned, and controlled by an adult with a named minor as a beneficiary. Funds in an ESA are available for varying education levels, from private elementary through graduate school, and the amount available for use depends solely on the underlying investment returns.

Contributions to a Coverdell ESA are made with after-tax dollars, and earnings grow on a tax-deferred basis until withdrawn. Withdrawals are tax-free when used on qualified education expenses, such as tuition, fees, books, and supplies. However, if a withdrawal is not used for educational purposes, the part representing account growth is subject to income taxes plus a 10 percent penalty.

The beneficiary must be under the age of eighteen at the time of plan creation, and the maximum annual contribution is $2,000 per beneficiary. Once the beneficiary turns eighteen, any additional contributions are subject to a 6 percent excise tax. Funds must be used before the beneficiary turns thirty, but if the beneficiary receives scholarships or decides not to pursue higher education, the funds can be transferred to another eligible family member without penalty.

Additionally, contributions to an ESA are not allowed for families whose household income is above $110,000 for a single filer or $220,000 for joint filers (as of 2023).

These accounts offer a wide range of investment options to select from and are attractive because they can be used for various educational expenses at any grade level. Unfortunately, the annual contribution limit of $2,000 and the income eligibility restrictions reduce their effectiveness as a college planning tool.

529 Savings Plan

A 529 Savings Plan is another tax-advantaged investment vehicle to help families save for future college expenses. These plans enable parents, grandparents, and other relatives or friends to contribute funds to a beneficiary's account. The account owner of a 529 Savings Plan is the legal owner of the account balance and always controls the distribution of any funds.

As with an ESA, earnings grow on a tax-deferred basis, and withdrawals are tax-free for qualified education expenses. The funds are suitable for accredited primary, secondary, and post-secondary institutions and cover tuition, fees, books, room, board, and other related expenses. However, withdrawals for non-educational expenses are subject to income taxes plus a 10% penalty on the withdrawal portion representing the underlying growth in value of the original contributions. Since no tax deductions exist for contributions, the portion of the withdrawal amount representing the original investments is returned without any tax implications.

These plans do not technically have a contribution limit but are subject to specific gifting rules described more in Chapter 19. In short, these rules allow an individual to contribute a tax-free gift of up to $85,000 as a single contribution during any five-year period. These plans have aggregate contribution limits that vary by state and typically range from $300,000 to $400,000. Unlike an ESA, there are no income limitations on one's ability to set up or make contributions.

As with ESAs, a 529 Savings Plan offers a range of investment options, with their performance determining the amount of money available for qualified educational expenses. In this regard, these savings plans do not offer any guarantees, like a prepaid plan. However, these funds can be used with a much greater degree of flexibility for any educational expense at any institution.

There is also no age limit on when the funds must be used, so these plans can continue to grow for decades, and the account beneficiary can be changed to another family member at any time. When my oldest son graduated from college, there was a residual balance in his 529 savings plan that we decided to maintain in the hopes of one day changing the beneficiary to his future children. In the meantime, the account continues to grow tax-deferred, making it a very powerful long-term college planning tool. In addition, starting in 2024, any unused balance can also fund annual Roth contributions for the beneficiary.

Summary

Starting early when saving for college is essential to maximizing the time available for investments to grow and compound. While no immediate federal tax savings exist for contributions, some states offer tax deductions or credits for contributions to plans within the state. Any withdrawals for qualified education expenses are tax-free, except for UTMA accounts.

A UTMA is the least favorable option for college savings since it offers no tax advantages on the underlying investment growth and gives complete account control to the beneficiary.

Prepaid college plans offer a fixed, known cost for future college expenses but have a variety of limitations on their usage. And while ESAs are a tax-advantaged and flexible option, their low contribution limits and income eligibility parameters limit their effectiveness as a college planning tool.

In our view, 529 Savings Plans offer the broadest flexibility, greatest parental control, and most significant potential opportunity to offset the full range of college expenses.

Chapter 16

Taxes

As Benjamin Franklin said, there are only two certainties in life: death and taxes. The effect of death can't be minimized, but your tax bill should be! The combination of income, state, employment, property, and sales taxes impacts every aspect of our daily lives. Despite the pervasive nature of taxation, it remains one of the most complex and misunderstood aspects of personal finance.

The average person will pay more than $500,000 in various taxes throughout their lifetime, representing about one-third of their total earnings! Let that sink in. The average person will send the government roughly one-third of all the money they earn in their lifetime.

Income taxes paid from work earnings alone represent 54 percent of this total liability. Real estate taxes comprise another 27 percent; the rest is a combination of state, local, property, or sales taxes.

The U.S. Tax Code contains the actual federal tax laws and is a 6,900-page labyrinth of rules and regulations. When tax regulations and official tax guidelines are included, it increases to about 75,000 pages. While it's nearly impossible to fully understand the nuances of that vast information, a basic appreciation for how taxes are calculated will help you make better financial decisions. This chapter describes the fundamental concepts impacting your income taxes and explains some of the most common deductions, income adjustments, and tax credits available.

Income

Calculating how much you owe in taxes starts with determining your total income. Regardless of the source, all the money you earn during a calendar year must be included on your tax return. The main categories of income are:

- **Wages, Salaries, and Tips**: Money made while working is considered earned income. These amounts are typically reported on either Form W-2 or Form 1099.

- **Interest**: This income is generated from interest-bearing accounts such as savings or money market accounts, certificates of deposit, or bonds. The amounts paid are reported on Form 1099-INT.

- **Dividends**: This type of income comes from owning shares in a company that pays a portion of its profits to its shareholders and is reported on Form 1099-DIV.

- **Retirement Income**: This category includes distributions from retirement accounts and pensions. These amounts are reported on Form 1099-R.

- **Social Security**: The amount you receive from Social Security is partially taxable if the total of your other income exceeds certain thresholds. Form 1099-SSA reports your Social Security earnings for the year.

- **Capital Gains and Losses**: These are generated from selling assets such as real estate, stocks, bonds, or mutual funds. If there is a profit, then it's a gain; otherwise, it's a loss. Form 1099B is used to report the details of these transactions.

- **Business Income**: As a business owner, you must report your income, whether through a partnership, company, or self-employed business.

- **Rental Income**: If you own investment property, you must report the income on your tax return.

All these items combined represent your total income. The forms used to report these various types of income will also include details on any taxes that were withheld and forwarded to the IRS during the year. These tax withholding amounts are designed to offset any tax liability as income is received.

There are a few things that aren't considered income, so make sure you don't report them as such:

- Something received as a gift

- Reimbursements and returns of deposits

- Life insurance proceeds that are paid upon the death of a loved one

- Various other assets one might inherit (Tax implications on receiving an inheritance are discussed in Chapter 20.)

Filing Status

The next step in understanding your tax situation is determining your filing status. Choosing the correct filing status is important because it can affect the amount of taxes owed and the eligibility for certain tax credits and deductions. The five types of filing statuses for income taxes are:

- **Single**: This status applies to individuals who are unmarried, divorced, or legally separated as of the last day of the calendar year.

- **Married Filing Jointly**: This category applies to married couples filing joint tax returns. Both spouses report their income, deductions, and credits on the same tax return. Married filing jointly applies if you are married as of the last day of the year. If your spouse passes away anytime during a calendar year, you would still be eligible to use this filing status for that year.

- **Married Filing Separately**: This classification applies to married couples filing separate tax returns. Each spouse reports their income, deductions, and credits on their respective tax returns. This option is used when couples want to maintain separate finances or avoid joint tax liability.

- **Head of Household**: This category applies to individuals who are unmarried and have supported at least one other individual for more than half of the tax year. The other individual must meet certain qualifying income thresholds and relationship tests to be considered a dependent for tax purposes.

- **Qualifying Widow(er) with Dependent Child**: This status applies to individuals who have lost their spouse within the past two years, have a dependent child, and meet other specific criteria.

Income Adjustments

Income adjustments can be applied to reduce one's total income for tax purposes. Subtracting these adjustments from total income results in one's Adjusted Gross Income or AGI. AGI is important because it helps determine taxpayers' eligibility for deductions and tax credits, as subsequently discussed in this chapter. There are four main types of income adjustments you may encounter.

- **Retirement Contributions**: Contributions to certain types of accounts help save for retirement and potentially reduce your AGI for tax purposes. You can contribute to a retirement account as long as you earn income from working. If you contribute to an employer-sponsored retirement plan, those amounts will already be reflected on your Form W-2 and won't require or create any additional adjustment on your tax return.

- **Student Loan Interest:** If you paid interest on a qualified student loan during the tax year, you may be able to subtract up to $2,500 of that interest from your AGI. This deduction can be especially helpful for recent graduates still paying off student loans. Unfortunately, this deduction is eliminated if your income is above certain levels.

- **Health Savings Account (HSA) Contributions:** HSAs are tax-advantaged accounts that can be used to pay for qualified medical expenses tax-free. Contributions to HSAs are tax-deductible and, therefore, reduce a person's income. HSAs can only be used in conjunction with a high-deductible health insurance plan but represent a valuable option to achieve tax savings on medical expenses.

- **Educator Expenses**: Teachers can reduce their taxable income by up to $300 a year for out-of-pocket purchases of classroom materials.

Deductions

Deductions are expenses taxpayers can subtract from their Adjusted Gross Income to determine their taxable income. Lowering taxable income is a top priority because it is the amount used to calculate your tax liability. Taxpayers can choose between itemizing their deductions or using the standard deduction.

The standard deduction is a fixed amount that varies depending on the taxpayer's filing status. For 2023, the standard deduction is:

- $13,850 for single filers

- $27,700 for joint filers

- $20,800 for head of household filers

- Those over the age of sixty-five can add $1,850 to this amount if filing single or $1,500 each if filing jointly.

In late 2017, revised tax codes nearly doubled the standard deduction and eliminated or vastly limited many itemized deductions. Therefore, more than 90 percent of Americans currently use the default standard deduction option.

Unfortunately, anyone wanting to increase their deduction by itemizing their expenses will find the eligible categories somewhat limited. In addition, the total amount of your itemized deductions must be greater than your standard deduction to make claiming your itemized deductions worthwhile. The main categories of itemized deductions are:

- **Medical Expenses**: Any money spent on medical-related costs can be included in this category, such as health insurance premiums, prescriptions, eyeglasses, hearing aids, and certain out-of-pocket expenses. Unfortunately, only the total expenses exceeding 7.5 percent of your Adjusted Gross

Income can be used as a deduction. For example, if a taxpayer's AGI is $100,000, they would need more than $7,500 of medical expenses to qualify, and then only the costs over this threshold would be deductible. Consequently, most find they cannot use their medical costs to help reduce their taxes.

- **State and Local Taxes**: This category includes state income taxes, sales taxes, and local taxes such as real estate taxes. Only a maximum of $10,000 can be used for this deduction, which limits its effectiveness.

- **Mortgage Interest**: If you have a mortgage on a primary or secondary residence, you can deduct the interest amount paid. This deduction only applies to interest paid on the first $750,000 of your aggregate mortgage amounts on either a primary or secondary home.

- **Charitable Contributions**: This is perhaps the most widely known deduction. Any gifts to a valid charity (sorry, that's not your kids!) can be deducted from your tax return. Keep track of those church donations and trips to Goodwill to take advantage of these potential tax savings.

Total Tax

The total tax owed to the government depends on your taxable income. This amount is calculated using a progressive tax bracket schedule that applies increasing tax rates as taxable income rises. Therefore, individuals who earn more income pay a higher percentage of taxes than those who earn less, as shown in the following table.

2023 Federal Tax Brackets			
Tax Bracket/Rate	Single	Married Filing Jointly	Head of Household
10%	$0 - $11,000	$0 - $22,000	$0 - $15,700
12%	$11,000 - $44,725	$22,001 - $89,450	$15,701 - $59,850
22%	$44,726 - $95,375	$89,451 - $190,750	$59,851 - $95,350
24%	$95,376 - $182,100	$190,751 - $364,200	$95,351 - $182,100
32%	$182,101 - $232,250	$364,201 - $462,500	$182,101 - $231,250
35%	$231,251 - $578,125	$462,501 - $693,750	$231,251 - $578,100
37%	$578,126+	$693,751+	$578,101+

This approach also applies to your own income as it accumulates throughout the year. You may start in one tax bracket, but if you earn extra income that pushes you into a higher tax bracket, only that additional portion is taxed at the higher income tax rate. For example, if you have taxable income of $40,000 as a single filer, you will owe:

- 10 percent on the first $11,000 or $1,100

- 12 percent on the remaining $29,000 or $3,480

- A total tax of $4,580 on a taxable income of $40,000, which equals 11.45 percent

Your average tax rate, or your effective rate, is the percentage of your taxable income that you actually paid in taxes (11.45 percent in the example above).

Your marginal tax rate is the highest tax rate you paid and only applies to the portion of income earned within that bracket (12 percent in the example above). It will always be higher than your effective or average rate.

Knowing both is important so that you have the most complete and accurate picture of your overall tax situation.

Tax Credits

Tax credits reduce the total taxes owed and are extremely valuable because they represent a dollar-for-dollar reduction in your tax liability. The main types of tax credits are described below.

- **Dependent Care Credit**: If you have children under thirteen or other dependents who require care while you work, you may be eligible for this credit. Depending on your income level, it can be as high as 35 percent of your qualifying expenses, with a maximum of $2,000 per child.

- **Retirement Savings Credit**: If you contribute to a retirement account such as an IRA or a 401(k) and your income is below certain thresholds, you may qualify for the retirement savings credit. This credit, up to 50 percent of your contributions with a maximum of $1,000 per person, can be a big boost for lower-income individuals trying to save for retirement.

- **Energy Credits**: If you make energy-efficient improvements to your home, such as installing solar panels or upgrading your insulation, you may be eligible for certain energy credits to help offset your improvement costs. In addition, tax credits are available for purchasing specific categories of electric vehicles.

- **Earned Income Tax Credit (EITC):** The EITC is a refundable tax credit for low- to moderate-income individuals and families. The credit amount varies depending on your income, filing status, and the number of qualifying children. In 2022, the maximum credit amount was $6,935 for a family with three or more qualifying children.

- **Child Tax Credit (CTC):** The CTC is a tax credit of up to $2,000 per child under seventeen. The credit is partially refundable, meaning that if the credit exceeds your tax liability, you may receive a refund for the difference.

- **Other Dependents Credit**: This credit is $500 for each eligible person a taxpayer supports during the year. Generally, this credit applies to children, students under twenty-four, and other qualifying relatives, such as elderly parents.

- **American Opportunity Tax Credit (AOTC):** The AOTC is a tax credit for qualified education expenses during the first four years of post-secondary education. The maximum credit amount is $2,500 per eligible student. The credit is partially refundable, meaning up to $1,000 of the credit may be refunded even if you don't owe any taxes.

- **Lifetime Learning Credit**: This credit of up to $2,000 per year per taxpayer is for qualified educational expenses in general. It is intended to help defray educational costs for those pursuing higher education to improve their job skills or acquire new ones. It also applies to courses that are not part of a degree program, such as certificate programs or trade schools.

It is important to note that these tax credits have very particular eligibility requirements. Be sure to research each thoroughly if you are trying to claim one (or consult a tax professional).

Taxes or Refund Owed

The taxes you owe are calculated by subtracting any taxes previously withheld from your income and any applicable tax credits from your total tax. You get a refund if the withholding and credit amounts exceed the total taxes. Otherwise, the amount owed is due on April 15 each year. If that date falls on a weekend or holiday, taxes are due on the next business day.

The IRS offers multiple payment options, including credit cards, debit cards, or direct debit from your bank account. If you can't pay your taxes in full by the due date, you can set up a payment plan with the IRS. You'll be charged interest and penalties if you don't pay on time. You may also owe additional taxes if the IRS determines you owe more than what was calculated when you filed.

The following calculation helps to summarize the steps involved in calculating your tax liability using the various concepts we have discussed:

Total Income
- Income Adjustments

Adjusted Gross Income
- Deductions

Taxable Income
x Tax Rate

Total Tax
- Withholding
- Tax Credit

Taxes or Refund Owed

Capital Gains and Dividends–A Special Tax Deal

Long-term capital gains and qualified dividends are taxed at lower rates than other income, making investments that produce dividends and capital gains more appealing. Remember, you can only spend what you make after paying taxes, so knowing which investment returns come with lower tax rates is essential.

Long-Term Capital Gains

Long-term capital gains are profits from the sale of assets held for more than a year, including real estate, stocks, mutual funds, or any other investment property or security type. The tax rate for long-term capital gains depends on the taxpayer's taxable income but starts as low as zero percent. That's right—0%—a pretty good tax rate! To qualify for that rate, you cannot be higher than the 12 percent income tax bracket or roughly $100,000

Adjusted Gross Income for a couple. In higher income tax brackets, the capital gains rate increases to 15 percent and expands to 20 percent for the highest possible income tax bracket. Those higher rates still represent significant savings over the applicable income tax rates.

To calculate your capital gain, you first need to determine the asset's cost basis. The cost basis is the original price paid for the asset plus any additional investments. These additions can include the reinvestment of prior profits, such as dividends, or the cost of any improvements made to a property. The cost basis is subtracted from the asset's sale price to determine if there was a gain or loss on the transaction.

For example, assume you initially invested $10,000 into mutual fund ABC. Over the next five years, mutual fund ABC paid dividends of $500 each year that you reinvested. Your original investment of $10,000 plus the $2,500 of total reinvested dividends would amount to a total cost basis of $12,500 for your mutual fund ABC. If you sold your investment for $15,000, you would have a capital gain of $2,500. If you sold mutual fund ABC for $10,000, you would have a loss of $2,500. A capital loss can be used to fully offset any other capital gains you had that year. If you still have extra losses, up to $3,000 can be used against other income in that tax year, and the remaining amount can be carried over for future use.

Qualified Dividends

Dividends must meet specific requirements to qualify for these preferential tax rates:

- The dividend must come from a U.S. corporation or certain foreign companies based in the United States.

- The shares on which the dividend is paid must be held for a defined duration, typically sixty days.

If a dividend does not satisfy these requirements, it is considered an ordinary dividend and taxed at regular income tax rates.

Selling Your Home

For most Americans, their single largest asset is their home. Special tax rules apply to the sale of your primary residence but have changed over the years.

Previously, you were allowed a one-time exemption to avoid paying taxes on the sale of a home if the next one was less expensive. This allowed people to downsize their homes once during their lifetime without tax implications.

In 1997, that approach was eliminated to give taxpayers more flexibility. With the new rule, you can avoid paying taxes on the sale of your appreciated primary residence if you meet specific residency requirements. If you have lived in a property as your primary residence for two of the preceding five years, you can exclude up to $500,000 of gains as a couple (or $250,000 as an individual) from your taxes. This is a very valuable tax savings option for homeowners.

Use Your Tax Return to Improve Your Finances

Far too often, people complete their tax return for the year and never bother to give it a second glance. This is understandable given the potential frustration of spending substantial time and effort to gather the necessary information and complete the return itself.

However, your tax return is an essential summary of your financial situation. It contains your total income and a good bit of your expenses, particularly if you itemize your deductions. It also serves as a guide to the future and forms the basis of tax-efficient retirement income planning.

A tax return is so important to one's financial plan that Nelson Financial Planning started in-house tax preparation services for its clients more than twenty years ago. Since then, our tax team has expanded to include four CPAs working with our clients each tax season. This year, we completed more than six hundred client tax returns. This helps our clients minimize their taxes and plan for the most tax-efficient retirement possible.

So, pull the tax return out of the file cabinet and take a second look at it.

- Did you get a refund, or did you owe money?

- Were you charged interest because you didn't pay enough taxes during the year?

- Did you maximize your retirement savings?

- Did you take advantage of doing a Qualified Charitable Distribution if you have a Required Minimum Distribution (more on that in the next chapter)?

- Was your Social Security fully or partially taxable (more on that in Chapter 18)?

- Did you take advantage of the preferential rate for qualified dividends and long-term capital gains?

That's just a few of the questions you should ask yourself as you stare at your tax return. Understanding your tax return is a crucial part of improving your finances.

For example, if you got a refund, then congratulations! You just gave the government an interest-free loan! If that refund exceeds $1,000, consider lowering your tax withholding on your paycheck or retirement income. That adjustment would put your money back in your own pocket, so you could decide what to do with it in the interim. Otherwise, you must wait until tax time to get your own money back from the government.

If you owe money, you should also make some changes because the IRS charges interest on any amounts owed. You can adjust your tax withholding at work and on your retirement or Social Security income to cover your taxes throughout the year rather than owing a considerable sum at tax time. Making quarterly tax payments is another way of ensuring you don't owe a large amount at tax time.

A Word About the Future

Tax rates will go up in 2026. This is not a prediction—it is a fact. The current marginal tax brackets of 12, 22, 24, 32, 35, and 37 percent represent temporary tax rates introduced in late 2017 for tax years 2018 through 2025. For the tax year 2026, these tax rates will become 15, 25, 28, 33, 35, and 39.6 percent, respectively. This tax increase shouldn't be a big surprise given Washington's need for additional income to offset the ballooning federal deficit. These forthcoming tax rate increases provide a significant planning opportunity for families.

- Should you realize certain income now to take advantage of the lower tax rates (e.g., selling stock that is worth more now than when you bought it)?

- Do you own real estate or a business that should be sold now rather than later?

- And, what about making gifts now instead of after your death (much more on that in Chapter 19)?

Understanding your taxes and having a perspective on the future will help you make a better financial plan!

Questions & Notes

Chapter 17

Retirement Accounts

Retirement accounts such as IRAs, 401(k)s, and 403(b)s are tax-advantaged savings options with no immediate tax implications on earnings. However, depending on your age, withdrawals from these accounts can spur tax consequences and penalties. Because of such limitations, they are often called qualified accounts.

Traditional IRA vs. Roth IRA

The Traditional IRA and the Roth IRA are individual retirement accounts (IRAs), allowing individuals to save directly for retirement on a tax-deferred basis, but with significant differences. A Traditional IRA permits tax-deductible contributions now, but withdrawals made during retirement are taxed as ordinary income. On the other hand, a Roth IRA allows after-tax contributions that are not tax deductible, but withdrawals occur tax-free during retirement.

Deciding Between Traditional or Roth IRA

One advantage of a Traditional IRA is that contributions reduce taxable income, thus lowering one's tax bill. This immediate financial boost provides additional money to invest for the future.

Traditional IRAs particularly benefit individuals expecting to be in a lower tax bracket during retirement. By having a lower tax rate during retirement, your tax-deductible contribution made at today's higher rate will save more money now than the expected tax cost for future withdrawals.

On the other hand, Roth IRAs offer tax-free withdrawals during retirement, which is advantageous for individuals who expect to be in a higher tax bracket during retirement or anticipate rising tax rates. Unlike Traditional IRAs, Roth IRAs do not require minimum distributions for individuals depending on age.

	Traditional IRA	Roth IRA
Pay Taxes	Later	Now
Growth	Tax Deferred	Potentially Tax-Free
Early Withdrawal	Penalty + Taxes	No penalty, but you may pay penalty + tax on earnings
After Age 59 ½		
Regular Withdrawals	Pay Taxes	Tax-Free
After Age 73		
Required Minimum Distributions	Yes	No

Roth IRAs are especially advantageous for younger investors. The younger you are and the lower your tax bracket, the more you should consider a Roth IRA over a Traditional one. This assumes you can afford to skip the current tax savings of lowering your tax bill from a traditional contribution. If your cash flow is limited and you need extra money to fund your retirement account, then the immediate tax savings of the Traditional IRA may make more sense. The chart on the left summarizes the main differences between Traditional and Roth IRAs.

Another factor in deciding between a Traditional IRA or a Roth IRA is that each has specific eligibility criteria based on income and availability of employer plans.

Eligibility Criteria for Each Type of IRA

Anyone with earned income from working is eligible to contribute to an IRA at any age. Previously, only those under seventy could contribute to an IRA. In recognition of longer life expectancies, that limitation was eliminated in 2019, allowing one to contribute to an IRA regardless of age.

Contribution Limits

An individual's contribution limit for Traditional and Roth IRAs is $6,500 for 2023, but you can invest it across either type as a combined limit. For example, you could put $2,000 in a Traditional IRA and $4,500 in a Roth (or any other combination not exceeding $6,500 in total). To account for inflation, the contribution limit is expected to increase to $7,000 in 2024. Individuals fifty and older can make an additional annual catch-up contribution of $1,000, which also automatically adjusts each year for inflation.

Deduction Eligibility

The eligibility criteria for deducting contributions to a Traditional IRA is quite complex, first depending on whether you are eligible to participate in an employer-sponsored plan, which is discussed later in this chapter.

If you are not eligible to participate in such a plan, then regardless of your income, you can contribute the

Traditional IRA Contribution Deduction Eligibility (for 2023)

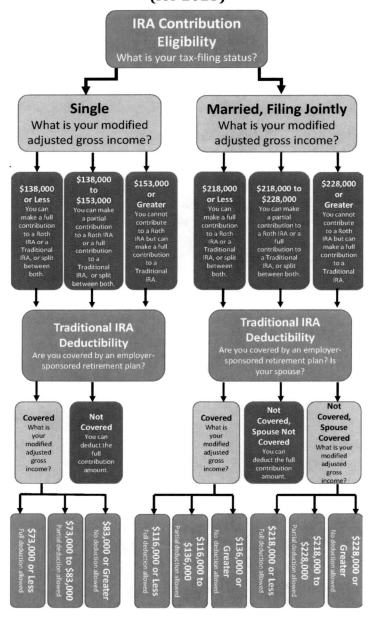

A full contribution equals 100 percent of earned income up to $6,500 for 2023 (plus $1,000 if you are fifty or older). Note: This information is intended to help you determine your contribution and tax-deduction eligibility for a Traditional IRA contribution. Certain limitations and definitions apply.

maximum amount to an IRA and receive a tax deduction for the entire contribution. If you or your spouse are eligible to participate in an employer plan, then income limits apply before you can take a tax deduction for your Traditional IRA contribution.

As the flow chart on the left shows, many factors determine your IRA contributions' tax deductibility.

Roth Income Limitations

Similarly, income limitations apply to one's ability to contribute to a Roth IRA. To fund a Roth IRA for 2023, your Modified Adjusted Gross Income (MAGI) must be less than $153,000 as a single filer or $228,000 as a joint filer.

Ensuring proper eligibility for a Traditional or Roth IRA contribution is complicated, so consult a tax professional or use reliable tax preparation software to avoid mistakes. This complexity is one reason we have a tax department at Nelson Financial Planning!

Roth Conversions

Some individuals start with a Traditional IRA and then convert their assets to a Roth IRA, referred to as a Roth conversion. While this can have numerous benefits, it has been misunderstood as a pathway to creating a tax-free retirement. Instead, a Roth conversion is a fully taxable event since you are converting pre-tax dollars to after-tax dollars.

When moving funds from a Traditional IRA to a Roth IRA, the converted amount is additional income that must be reported on your tax return for that year. This extra income increases your tax bill and potentially creates further tax consequences in other parts of your return. In addition, paying the subsequent tax bill reduces your available cash for investing elsewhere.

While a tax-free retirement sounds good, nothing comes free, so you may be surprised at the taxes owed upfront to get there. Consequently, a conversion must be carefully planned to address the numerous potential tax issues. We recommend having a tax professional complete a tax return projection before any conversion to fully understand its cost.

Employer-Sponsored Plans

Employer-sponsored plans are retirement savings plans offered by employers to their employees. Participation is voluntary, but after December 31, 2024, it becomes mandatory for new employer plans, with auto-enrollment requiring at least a 3 percent contribution unless an employee opts out.

The Power of Matching Contributions

Employers often incentivize employee participation by matching contributions as an employee benefit. If you work for an employer who offers to match some of your contributions, I compel you to participate! Fully contributing the amount necessary ensures you receive the entire employer match provided. If you don't, you're just throwing away free money!

Suppose you make $40,000 per year, and your employer matches 50 percent of your contributions up to 6 percent. If you contribute $2,400 per year (less than $100 per bi-weekly pay period), you would receive an extra $1,200 in matching contributions from your employer.

If you struggle to make ends meet, remember the pay yourself first principle when you next receive a salary increase. Contribute that extra amount to your employer's retirement plan so you don't leave free money from your employer on the table. Just one year of receiving $1,200 could turn into nearly $20,000 over 30 years, assuming a 9 percent return!

Vesting Periods

Employers who offer matching contributions also enact vesting schedules, which limit employees' ownership of an employer's contributions until they work there for a certain number of years. For example, a vesting schedule that lasts 4 years passes on 25 percent of the employer's contributions each year to the employee for four years before the employee wholly owns them. In contrast, you always fully own your direct employee contributions.

Plan Limits and Types

Employer retirement plans allow employees to make either pre-tax or after-tax contributions with higher contribution limits than IRAs. Pre-tax or traditional contributions come with immediate tax savings, while after-tax or Roth contributions have tax savings as you withdraw funds in retirement.

For 2023, the contribution limit for these employer plans is $22,500 per year, with an additional $7,500 catch-up contribution option for employees over fifty. These limits are indexed for inflation and typically increase each year. Starting in 2026, the catch-up contribution amount will only be available for Roth accounts of employees making more than $145,000 in the previous year.

Several employer-sponsored plans exist, including 401(k), 403(b), and 457 plans.

- **A 401(k) plan** is generally offered by private or public for-profit companies.

- **A 403(b) plan** is offered to employees of non-profit organizations, such as schools and hospitals.

- **A 457 plan** is offered to government employees and is considered a deferred compensation plan. This unique deferral feature allows an employee who retires to withdraw funds at any age without facing an early withdrawal tax penalty.

- **A SEP-IRA** is an employer plan option available to self-employed individuals with contribution limits based on that person's net earnings.

Investment Options

Take the time to review all investment options within your plan to create the asset allocation that works best for you. Sometimes, employer-sponsored plans have limited investment options and offer predominantly target date funds. As discussed in Chapter 9, target date fund options offer a cookie-cutter approach and typically become too conservative earlier than is necessary for most employees. To improve your investment results, carefully evaluate all the available choices inside the employer plan and look for those options with solid, long-term track records and low expenses.

Rolling Over Employment Plans

When you leave your employer, you should take your money with you. Just as you wouldn't leave your family photo on your former desk, you shouldn't leave your money behind. Rolling over an employer plan to an IRA has several benefits:

- Greater flexibility and control over your money, as IRAs offer a more comprehensive range of investment choices

- Ability to consolidate retirement savings into a single account, streamlining the management and tracking of retirement funds

- Increased distribution options for your beneficiaries that are detailed in the Inherited IRA section later in this chapter

Florida Retirement System Options

As a Florida-based firm, we've included a brief discussion about retirement plans available to employees of the state's largest employer, the State of Florida. The Florida Retirement System, or FRS, offers three different options from which employees can choose.

Pension Plan

This traditional defined benefit plan generates a guaranteed monthly retirement check based on years of service and average final compensation.

Investment Plan

This plan converts your expected pension amount into a lump sum of money you can invest and manage like a private employer 401(k) plan. Under this option, you do not receive a pre-determined monthly check, but rather, your potential retirement income depends on how well your underlying investments perform. While the Investment Plan provides a broader potential to leave retirement money to your family, it lacks the income guarantee of the Pension Plan.

Deferred Retirement Option Program

The third choice for State of Florida employees is the Deferred Retirement Option Program or DROP. This alternative combines the guaranteed monthly retirement check of the Pension Plan with the ability to continue working for the state—all while your pension check accrues each month in a separate DROP account, which currently earns 4 percent interest.

Selecting a Plan

Because these options vary immensely, it's essential to clearly understand and closely compare each plan to select the one appropriate for you. Consider the many details and differences when making your retirement election under the Florida Retirement System.

With so many parts and pieces factoring into your decision, we created a separate booklet with a deeper explanation.

Initially published in 2015, *The State of Your Retirement: The Essential Guide for all State of Florida Employees* by Joel Garris is now in its fifth edition and provides an in-depth look at these FRS choices.

If you are a State of Florida employee or know someone who is, download your free copy of this booklet by scanning the QR code below or visiting our website.

www.NelsonFinancialPlanning.com

FRS Booklet

Retirement Account Withdrawals

Withdrawing money from a retirement account in the most tax-efficient manner requires understanding the different factors and situations that vary by account type and timing. For example, withdrawals from traditional retirement accounts are taxed as ordinary income. In contrast, Roth IRA withdrawals are tax-free.

Regular withdrawals that are made during retirement years are not subject to any tax penalty as long as they occur after age fifty-nine and a half. Early withdrawals are those made before fifty-nine and a half and are typically subject to an additional 10 percent penalty.

Early Withdrawal Penalty Exceptions

There are several exceptions that exempt the penalty for an early withdrawal. These include:

- Specific, qualified purposes
- Regular, established income payments
- Early retirement scenarios

If the money is used for specific, qualified purposes, early withdrawals may be penalty-free. The most common scenarios are:

- Paying for qualified higher education expenses
- Withdrawals for those living in federally declared disaster areas up to $22,000
- Making a downpayment of up to $10,000 on a first home
- Paying for unreimbursed medical expenses above 7.5 percent of your AGI or health insurance premiums while unemployed
- Withdrawals after becoming disabled

Also, establishing regular income from your IRA can help avoid the 10 percent early withdrawal penalty. The penalty exemption for a series of substantially equal periodic payments exists under Section 72(t) of the IRS code.

Other exceptions apply in specific early retirement scenarios, such as:

- **Retiring at age Fifty-Five or Older:** You may withdraw funds directly from your employer's sponsored plan without early withdrawal penalties.

- **Retiring from Specific High-Risk Jobs:** Employees such as law enforcement officers or firefighters who retire over fifty can make penalty-free withdrawals from a qualified employer plan.

Special Roth Exceptions

Roth IRAs are treated very differently because original contributions can be withdrawn tax- and penalty-free at any age. However, once all your initial contributions have been withdrawn, the remaining earnings from your Roth IRA may be taxable and subject to the 10 percent penalty as an early withdrawal if you are under the age of fifty-nine and a half.

However, if you use the distribution for one of the early withdrawal exceptions mentioned previously, you can avoid the 10 percent penalty, but the earnings portion of the withdrawal is subject to ordinary income tax.

A special exception exists in the case of a distribution from a Roth that you have owned for more than five years for a disability or a downpayment of up to $10,000 for a first-time home. In these two limited situations, you can avoid the 10 percent penalty, and the earnings are tax-free!

Required Minimum Distributions (RMDs)

RMDs are withdrawals retirement account owners must make annually once they reach seventy-three. This age is scheduled to increase to seventy-five in the year 2033. Roth IRAs do not have any RMD requirements.

How to Calculate

The RMD amount is based on the individual's age and total retirement account balance. To calculate the proper amount, divide the account balance at the start of the year by the life expectancy factor the IRS established for your age in that particular year.

This required withdrawal can be made at any time or in any sequence during a calendar year, as long as the total amount of the RMD is withdrawn by year-end.

The only exception is if the retirement monies exist in an employer-sponsored plan where the individual still works. These account balances are subject to RMD rules only after that individual leaves that employer.

Penalties and Taxes

Failure to take the RMD can result in a penalty of 25 percent of the amount to be withdrawn, plus applicable income taxes. While this penalty decreased from 50 percent in late 2022, it remains one of the most significant tax penalties in the IRS code. A taxpayer can further reduce this liability to 10 percent if they withdraw a missed required distribution within two years.

Regardless, we recommend taking your RMD every year and automating the calculation and distribution to avoid tax penalties. Remember, these RMDs also apply to inherited or beneficiary IRAs, which we will discuss later in this chapter.

RMDs and Qualified Charitable Distributions

Qualified Charitable Distributions (QCDs) are one of the most valuable tax-saving options for charitable-minded individuals regarding their RMDs. By making a required distribution payable directly to a qualified charity, the reportable income from your RMD is reduced on a dollar-for-dollar basis, creating a tax-free QCD.

Also, your donations can exceed your RMD, resulting in additional tax savings, as long as the total amount donated doesn't exceed $100,000 per person per year. QCDs can occur any time after seventy and a half on regular and inherited retirement accounts, so you can make QCDs before reaching your RMD starting age.

RMDs and Inherited IRAs

An inherited IRA is received by a named beneficiary, such as a spouse, child, or another individual, after the original IRA owner passes away. The distribution rules for inherited or beneficiary IRAs depend on the relationship between the beneficiary and the original IRA owner and the original IRA owner's age at the time of death. While no early distribution penalties exist on withdrawals from an inherited IRA, distribution rules apply to inherited traditional IRAs and Roth IRAs.

Surviving Spouse Beneficiary

If the beneficiary is a surviving spouse, they can maintain it as a separate inherited IRA or combine it with their own IRA. If treated as an inherited IRA, specific distribution rules apply. But when combined with their own IRA, the only distribution rule that applies is the usual RMD that starts at age seventy-three.

Non-Spouse Beneficiary

Prior to 2020, the distribution schedule for inherited accounts was described as a stretch IRA because distributions could be stretched over the beneficiary's lifetime, thereby creating a powerful tax-deferred vehicle that could potentially last for decades.

Unfortunately, for retirement accounts inherited after January 1, 2020, a total payout of these inherited accounts must now occur within ten years (this is known as the 10-year rule). This means you must take out the entire account balance by the end of the tenth year following the year of death of the IRA owner. The 10-year rule applies to inherited traditional and Roth IRAs. This requirement substantially accelerates the tax implications of inheriting a retirement account and significantly reduces what used to be a very flexible and tax-beneficial distribution schedule.

In addition to the 10-year rule, inherited IRAs for non-spouse beneficiaries may also be subject to annual RMDs. If the original IRA owner was seventy-three or older when they passed, the non-spouse beneficiary must take RMDs from the inherited IRA starting by December 31 of the year following the original IRA owner's death. The amount of any required minimum distribution is based on the beneficiary's life expectancy and the balance of the inherited IRA.

However, if the original owner was less than seventy-three when they passed, then the beneficiary does not need to observe any required annual distribution so long as the entire account balance is paid out in ten years. In addition, certain exceptions to these distribution rules apply to eligible designated beneficiaries who are disabled, minors, or less than ten years younger than the original owner.

These rules for inherited or beneficiary IRAs can be quite complex, particularly with the accelerated ten-year payout schedule. Waiting until that tenth year to develop your withdrawal strategy will likely create a significant tax liability. Chapter 20 includes examples for effectively managing inherited retirement accounts, but we recommend that individuals who inherit an IRA engage in extensive planning to ensure the most tax-efficient distribution strategy.

Retirement Income Planning

Generating income from investment accounts to provide money for retirement is a highly specialized process. Retirement income planning depends on a variety of factors, including an individual's financial needs, tax situation, and other sources of retirement income. It is essential to consider all these points when deciding to take withdrawals and from which accounts they should be taken.

At Nelson Financial Planning, we typically start mapping out an individual's retirement income strategy a few years before actual retirement. That way, we help ensure your retirement income comes to you as tax-efficiently as possible.

Chapter 18

Social Security

Social Security is a government program providing financial assistance to individuals who are retired, disabled, or have lost a loved one. Established in 1935 as part of President Franklin D. Roosevelt's New Deal, Social Security was designed to provide a safety net for Americans struggling during the Great Depression.

Today, it pays over $1.1 trillion in annual benefits to approximately 70 million beneficiaries (about 21 percent of the U.S. population). On the other hand, in 2000, 49 million people (less than 16 percent of the U.S. population) collected some form of Social Security. This nearly 43 percent increase in beneficiaries is accompanied by a significant decline in workers contributing to Social Security.

- In 1945, there were almost forty-two workers for every beneficiary.

- By 1950, that number had dropped to seventeen.

- Today, there are less than three workers for every beneficiary.

This increase in beneficiaries and decrease in current workers underscore the ongoing concerns about Social Security's long-term viability.

The Purpose and Reality of Social Security

Social Security was never intended to cover all living expenses during retirement but rather to provide income to the neediest populations. Today, the average Social Security benefit represents about 40 percent of most Americans' pre-retirement income. That remaining 60 percent is your responsibility, so we wrote this book to help.

Unfortunately, Social Security is the largest source of income for most beneficiaries, with an average benefit at one's full retirement age in 2023 of $1,800 per month. Among 40 percent of retirees, it provides more than half their household income. For about 15 percent of the population, it provides nearly all their income in retirement.

Social Security Funding

Generally, anyone who earns a paycheck contributes to Social Security, as the primary funding sources for Social Security are:

- Payroll taxes from current workers

- Matching taxes from employers

- Asset reserves in the Social Security trust fund (around $2.9 trillion)

Payroll taxes are only collected from earned income, not retirement or investment income. The current payroll tax that funds Social Security is 12.4 percent, with 6.2 percent coming from employees and the other 6.2 percent from their employers. Self-employed individuals must pay the entire tax amount since they are both the employee and employer.

Contributions are limited by a wage cap indexed for inflation that increases annually. As of 2023, payroll contributions only apply to the first $160,200 of individual earnings. This means no Social Security taxes are paid on an individual's annual earnings exceeding $160,200.

Calculating Social Security Benefits

Several factors can affect an individual's Social Security benefit amount. The primary determinant is your earnings history; the second is when you start collecting it. Individuals may also qualify for different types of Social Security based on extenuating circumstances (like disability or the passing of a loved one) outlined in the subsequent section.

Earnings, Credits, and Retirement Age

The amount of Social Security benefits an individual is entitled to receive in retirement is based on their earning history, which is the amount of money earned through various jobs over one's lifetime. The Social Security Administration (SSA) records an individual's earnings throughout their lifetime and uses an average of earnings over the highest thirty-five years, adjusted for inflation. The more money you make along the way, the higher your Social Security benefit amount.

To qualify for any Social Security benefits, you must have a total of forty credits, which are accrued as you work. One credit is earned by making at least $1,640 (as of 2023) in a particular calendar quarter. Effectively, you must work for at least ten years to be eligible for any benefit.

The SSA uses a formula to calculate an individual's primary insurance amount (PIA), which is the amount of money an individual is entitled to receive at their full retirement age (FRA). For those born before 1960, the FRA ranges from sixty-five to sixty-seven years old; after 1960, the FRA is sixty-seven.

The age at which an individual chooses to retire directly impacts their Social Security benefit amount. If you take Social Security before your FRA, your benefits are permanently reduced. Conversely, they increase if you wait to collect benefits past your FRA (up until age seventy). Your work history (i.e., the employers you worked for over time) can also have an impact because Social Security does not cover some public sector jobs.

Social Security Benefit Types

Four main types of Social Security benefits are designed with different intents and eligibility requirements.

Retirement Benefits

Retirement benefits account for nearly 85 percent of all benefits paid by Social Security. To be eligible for retirement benefits, an individual must be at least sixty-two years old; however, choosing to retire and collect Social Security at that age permanently reduces the benefit amount. The decision to take retirement benefits early, therefore, should be carefully considered.

This reduction is calculated by multiplying the number of months the individual has until their FRA and multiplying that by 5/9 percent. For example, at sixty-three, with an FRA of sixty-seven, you still have forty-eight months before your FRA. Multiplying 48 months by 5/9 of a percent is 26.7 percent. This means your Social Security retirement benefit at age sixty-three would be 26.7 percent less than if you waited until sixty-seven. In contrast, after your FRA, your benefit increases 8 percent each year that you delay collecting (until you reach seventy). Beyond age seventy, there is no additional increase in your benefit except for annual cost of living adjustments.

Disability Benefits

To be eligible for disability benefits, an individual must meet the SSA's definition of disability. This means they must have a medical condition that prevents them from working and is either expected to last at least one year or result in death. These benefits are intended to provide financial assistance to individuals unable to support themselves due to their disability. Disability benefits amount to about 14 percent of the benefits that Social Security pays.

Survivor Benefits

To be eligible for survivor benefits, an individual must be the surviving spouse, child, or parent of a deceased worker eligible for Social Security benefits. These benefits are intended to provide financial assistance to people who have lost a loved one and are struggling to make ends meet. The survivor must also satisfy certain age and relationship requirements.

Generally, a spouse must be sixty to collect these benefits under their loved one's Social Security record. A significant issue with survivor benefits arises when a spouse passes. If both individuals were collecting Social Security retirement benefits, only the larger benefit amount would continue as a survivor benefit. The lesser benefit amount ceases, resulting in a drop in household income for the surviving spouse.

Family Benefits

To be eligible for family benefits, an individual must be the spouse or child of an individual collecting retirement or disability Social Security benefits. A spouse can collect these benefits if they are caring for a child who is disabled or under sixteen. For a child to collect benefits directly, they must be disabled or under eighteen (nineteen if still in high school). Family and survivor benefits account for about 1 percent of all Social Security payments.

When Should I Take Social Security?

Choosing when to take Social Security is a highly individualized decision that depends on many factors. In making this decision, consider these general guidelines.

The Earlier You Take It, the Less It Is

Do you remember the example we used earlier in this chapter? If you take Social Security retirement benefits at sixty-three and your FRA is sixty-seven, your benefits would be 26.7 percent less. It's easy to think the optimal solution is delaying Social Security for as long as possible, but you must analyze your situation to determine the best approach.

Start by calculating the time it will take to recover the total amount you would have received had you started earlier. Compare that total amount of benefits to the extra amount you would get by waiting. The payback period, or amount of time it takes for that extra monthly amount to add up to the total amount you could have received by starting earlier, is often ten to twelve years.

For example, if your Social Security benefit at age sixty-seven is $2,000 per month and the reduced amount at age sixty-three is $1,466 (or 26.7 percent less), you gave up 48 months of $1,466 or $70,368 while you were waiting until age sixty-seven to start collecting. To recoup that total amount, it would take nearly 11 years of collecting the extra $534 to accumulate that same $70,368. That's a long time, especially considering that inflation will reduce the value of those dollars later.

Additionally, retirees typically need more money earlier because younger individuals are generally more active, and being more active often results in needing more money to pay for activities!

Delaying Will Increase It

Your retirement benefit amount increases by 8 percent each year after reaching your FRA, so you collect about 24 percent more at age seventy than at age sixty-seven. We often recommend this option when one hasn't saved enough for retirement. The decision to take Social Security retirement benefits at any age requires a thoughtful consideration of your overall financial picture.

Beware of Taking It if You Are Still Working!

If you elect to take Social Security before reaching your FRA, your benefit is reduced by $1 for every $2 in employment income above $21,240 as of 2023. This earnings limit increases slightly every year, but if you plan to work before reaching your FRA, you must be careful about triggering a payback of your Social Security benefits. Bottom line: if you are still working and younger than your FRA, you should wait until you stop working (or reduce your amount of working) to start collecting Social Security.

We are All Living Longer

As we mentioned, you should prepare for retirement to last at least twenty years as the average life expectancy continues to rise. Your Social Security benefit amount at the beginning of retirement is permanent, with any future cost of living increases based on this amount. In addition, this directly impacts the potential benefits your spouse receives when you pass because the surviving spouse only receives the higher benefit, and the lesser benefit stops.

Social Security is Taxable!

Many people believe that Social Security benefits aren't taxable because they represent a return of payroll taxes already collected on their earned income throughout their lifetime. Unfortunately, that is not the case anymore.

Starting in 1984, Social Security benefits became subject to federal income tax. The amount of your Social Security benefits included in your adjusted gross income is based on the combined total of all your other income. The thresholds for triggering Social Security taxation start at $25,000 for single filers and $32,000 for married couples. These low-income thresholds have never been indexed for inflation. Consequently, every year, more people pay taxes on their Social Security benefits.

Will It Still Be There?

Everywhere you look, you see stories that Social Security is running out of money. At its current trajectory, the Social Security trust fund is projected to run out of money in 2035. However, that doesn't mean Social Security will not have funds available.

Social Security benefits are paid through payroll taxes and the $2.9 trillion Social Security trust fund. Every American worker and employer will continue paying payroll taxes. Thus, Social Security will have money to pay its promised benefits, but at a reduced amount. If the trust fund runs out of money, benefits will decline by about 20 percent.

The reality is that Social Security has been in crisis before. In the late 70s and early 80s, the Social Security program paid out more than was collected for several years before politicians found the willpower to address the issue. Over time, a variety of solutions have shored up the program that we expect to see again:

- **Raise the Retirement Age.** We see this as a realistic option, but only for people at least fifteen to twenty years away from collecting, providing enough time to adjust retirement plans.

- **Increase the Tax Rate.** The tax rate could increase from its current level of 6.2 percent (which started at 1 percent and has gradually risen over time).

- **Raise the Wage Cap.** The limit on wages subject to Social Security tax increases every year. Twenty years ago, this wage cap was around $80,000; today, it's doubled to over $160,000.

These are just some of the adjustments we expect to see in the years ahead that could help stabilize Social Security. It is undoubtedly a vital program, providing regular income to millions of Americans.

However, Social Security was never intended to be anyone's sole source of income in retirement, so proper planning for your future on your terms has never been more critical. A couple of key questions to start considering include the following:

- How much will your Social Security be?

- What other income will you have in retirement?

- How much will you rely on Social Security as a source of income for your retirement?

To determine your expected Social Security benefits, visit ssa.gov. After setting up an account, you can view your earnings record and potential benefits at various ages.

Questions & Notes

Chapter 19

Death: The Other Certainty

The other certainty of life, besides taxes, is death. Nobody gets out of the game of life alive. And, no matter how much you plan, you will never fully appreciate the emotional toll your death will have on your loved ones. My saddest moments have been consoling someone whose life has been shattered by the passing of a spouse, parent, or child. These conversations grow even more difficult when the loved one's estate and finances were not adequately planned. Unfortunately, many misconceptions complicate estate planning, so it is not an uncommon scenario. This chapter provides an overview of the most critical concepts to understand and common pitfalls to avoid when transferring property after you pass.

How Property Passes

Property is any physical or intangible item that can be officially owned or possessed by an individual or entity. Tangible property includes assets such as land and buildings, while intangible property includes financial assets and intellectual property. These two classifications of assets transfer at death to a beneficiary in three ways: by operation of law, operation of contract, or by a will.

Each of these three transfer methods has different estate planning implications, discussed in more detail below.

Personal property is slightly different because these assets can be physically touched, transported, and transferred from one location to another. This type of property includes items such as furniture, vehicles, electronics, and jewelry and can only be transferred at death to a named person by a will.

Operation of Law

Transferring property at one's death by operation of law refers to the automatic reassignment of ownership according to the pertinent legal principles or statutes without the need for specific action or agreement between the parties.

When a property transfers to someone by operation of law based on how that asset is titled, the transfer is automatic, regardless of what is stipulated in any other document or will. There is no room for debate or adjustment; under the operation of law, the title on the property takes precedence over everything else. So, if you verbally tell your son he is going to get your house when you die, but your daughter is listed as the joint owner on the title, then your daughter will get the house. There are four main ways property can be titled.

- **Individual**: This type of ownership means one individual owns the property and has complete control over what happens to it at their passing. This titling results in property passing to another based on the terms of that individual's will or the relevant state laws of intestacy (more on what that means later in this chapter).

- **Joint Tenancy with Rights of Survivorship (JTWROS)**: This titling allows for two or more owners to hold an undivided interest in the property. Upon the death of any owner, the entire property automatically transfers to the remaining owner(s). The last person remaining will own the entire interest in the property.

- **Tenancy in Common**: This titling also allows for two or more owners but provides for unequal shares among them. Each person owns a separate and distinct interest in the property. On the death of any owner, their respective share is transferred based on that owner's will or the laws of intestacy.

- **Tenancy by the Entirety**: This type of ownership involves married couples when, at the death of one spouse, the total ownership automatically transfers to the surviving spouse. With this titling, neither individual can transfer or dispose of the property without the consent of the other. This registration also provides a layer of creditor protection for married couples. A creditor of one spouse cannot make a claim against an asset titled as a tenancy by the entirety unless both spouses are subject to the same creditor liability. In Florida, a JTWROS automatically creates a tenancy by the entirety if the two owners are married.

Operation of Contract

The process of transferring property by operation of contract involves naming beneficiaries directly in the asset's title or account registration. Retirement account custodial agreements and insurance contracts provide owners with the option of naming beneficiaries as part of the underlying agreements governing such property. Trust agreements also function as contracts based on their specific distribution provisions.

Automatic Transfer or Payment on Death

For some types of property, such as regular investments or bank accounts, owners can add a Transfer on Death (TOD) or Payable on Death (POD) addendum to the account registration. This serves as a contract between the asset owner and the holding institution that is legally binding. At the death of the owner, the property will automatically transfer to the named beneficiaries.

Extra caution and diligence must be taken with TOD and POD registrations to avoid unintended consequences if named beneficiaries are not kept up to date. Once you pass, there are no options for changing the beneficiaries, and it automatically transfers to whoever is listed on the account registration.

The worst scenario I have witnessed involved an ex-spouse who was still named as the beneficiary of a life insurance policy. Needless to say, the current spouse was less than pleased, but there was absolutely nothing that could be done to change the named beneficiary.

In Florida, owners of real property (real estate such as land and buildings) can use an enhanced life estate registration to establish a TOD on the applicable real property to transfer its ownership after their death without the necessity for probate. Beneficiaries named in the registration (or any other account that operates by contract) have no ownership rights to the property until the owner or owners pass. This type of registration is also known as a Ladybird Deed, named after former First Lady Lady Bird Johnson, who used this technique in her estate planning.

Beneficiaries

Beneficiaries can be named as primary or contingent beneficiaries. Primary beneficiaries are first in line to own the property when the owners pass. Contingent beneficiaries are only entitled to ownership if the primary beneficiaries have predeceased the asset owner. Beneficiaries can also be named as per stirpes or per capita.

- **Per stirpes** means that the beneficiary's share of the property is divided equally among that beneficiary's heirs. Stirpes is Latin for by branch, so in essence, this type of designation follows the bloodline or direct descendants of a beneficiary.

- **Per capita** provides for distribution among a named group. If two beneficiaries are named per capita and one of them predeceased the property owner, the surviving beneficiary will be the sole beneficiary.

Most importantly, naming beneficiaries on any asset allows it to pass directly to the beneficiaries without having to go through probate (see below for more details on what this involves). The ownership change is automatic upon the death of the owner(s). We recommend checking your named beneficiaries a minimum of every two years to make sure the individuals named are still the ones you want to receive that property. You don't want any unintended consequences you can't fix after you die!

Operation of Will

A will is a legal document that specifies how a person's assets are to be distributed after they pass. A will typically identifies someone as an executor or personal representative to carry out the terms of the will. The provisions of a will only take effect upon one's death and only impact those assets that have not passed to others through the operation of law or the operation of contract. Assets that typically pass through a will are those that were in that individual's name only.

The Limitations of Wills

Most people don't realize that a will is always subject to probate. As a legal process, probate is designed to validate the decedent's will, identify heirs, and oversee the transfer procedure. Having a will does not avoid probate; instead, it serves as a roadmap, providing direction throughout the often costly, lengthy, and time-consuming probate process.

Having a will only avoids dying intestate, which means dying without leaving any direction on who gets your assets. If you die intestate, then all your assets will be disbursed based on the hierarchy of beneficiaries set forth in the laws of your state.

If you don't want state laws determining who gets what when you pass, then make sure you have a valid will. If you want to minimize your heirs' exposure to the costly and time-consuming legal probate process, then take the time to check the titles and account registration of any property and assets you own and add beneficiaries whenever possible. This ensures those assets aren't tied to a will and the probate process. Be sure to review all bank accounts, real estate, investment and retirement accounts.

Besides a will, there are three other estate planning documents you should have. However, all three documents are only valid while you are alive and cease to have any impact when you die.

Power of Attorney

A Power of Attorney (POA) is a legal document granting someone (known as the agent or attorney-in-fact) the authority to act on behalf of someone else (the principal) in legal and financial matters. It is typically used when the grantor (or principal) is unable or unavailable to manage their own affairs due to illness, absence, or other circumstances. Powers of attorney can be general, granting broad authority to the agent, or limited to a specific purpose or timeframe.

They are also considered either durable or springing. A durable POA is effective immediately, regardless of the mental state of the principal. Therefore, great care must be exercised in choosing an agent with a durable power of attorney, as it takes effect the moment the principal signs it. If you have any reservations about your selected agent, choose someone else!

A springing POA is effective only upon the occurrence of a specified event, such as the incapacity of the principal. A springing POA, however, can sometimes create issues with proving the occurrence of such event.

Health Care Surrogate

A Health Care Surrogate (HCS) is a legal document appointing another person to make medical decisions on behalf of someone else, often referred to as a medical power of attorney. The agent is entrusted with ensuring the principal's medical wishes and preferences are respected and followed. This authority is essential when the principal is incapacitated or unable to communicate their own decisions.

Living Will

This document covers more limited medical decisions relating to end-of-life wishes. It outlines the type of medical interventions the principal would like to receive (or not) regarding life-sustaining treatments, such as resuscitation, mechanical ventilation, artificial nutrition, and hydration.

Trusts: A Totally Separate Animal!

A trust is a contract that details specific terms regarding holding property for the benefit of an individual. Accordingly, assets passing to a beneficiary under a trust do so under the operation of contract principles, as previously discussed. The parties to a trust include the grantor who establishes the trust, the trustee whose job it is to manage the trust assets, and the beneficiary who receives the benefits of the trust. Depending on the type of trust, the same or different individuals can serve all three roles.

The trust document outlines the terms and conditions under which the trustee manages and distributes the assets. It specifies how the assets should be used, when and how they should be distributed to the beneficiaries, and any other instructions or restrictions set forth by the grantor. In essence, the trust terms create the plan of action for the trust assets.

One of the keys to using any trust effectively is to make sure any assets of the trust are appropriately re-registered and titled in the trust name. This process is known as funding the trust. This is one of the most overlooked steps in the proper utilization of trusts. If assets are not titled in the exact name of the trust, then the provisions of the trust don't apply, rendering the trust meaningless.

Trusts can be either revocable or irrevocable. Each type of trust has its own unique characteristics and countless variations within each category.

Revocable Trusts

This type of trust is perhaps the most common and is created during one's lifetime. It allows the grantor to maintain control of their assets during their lifetime and provides flexibility to modify or revoke the trust. A revocable living trust is simply an extension of the grantor and, as such, typically uses the grantor's Social Security number as its own tax identification number. Accordingly, any taxable transaction or activity inside these trusts passes through to the grantor's individual tax return.

A common misconception is that revocable trusts protect against any liability or creditors of the individuals setting up these trusts. Unfortunately, there is no such protection during the lifetime of the grantor because a revocable trust can be modified or revoked during the grantor's life. It is only when the grantor passes that a revocable trust becomes irrevocable and, thereby, creditor-proof. The key benefit of these trusts is avoiding probate, which simplifies the transfer process and provides greater privacy since trust terms remain confidential and are not subject to any court proceedings.

Irrevocable Trusts

As the name suggests, an irrevocable trust cannot be modified or revoked, which offers beneficiaries protection from creditors. It also provides the grantor the opportunity to specifically dictate the future use of their assets to prevent irresponsible spending, mismanagement, or poor behavior choices by beneficiaries. Irrevocable trusts require their own taxpayer identification number, which necessitates the annual filing of a separate trust tax return.

The most common types of irrevocable trusts include those typically used for estate planning purposes.

- **Credit shelter or marital trusts** provide for estate tax avoidance, as discussed below.
- **Testamentary trusts** are created through wills, take effect on the grantor's death, and are often used for minor children.
- **Special needs trusts** provide financial assistance to individuals with disabilities while preserving their eligibility for government benefits by allowing the trust assets to supplement, rather than replace, public assistance.

In recent years, the use of irrevocable trusts to qualify for Medicaid and related nursing home care benefits has increased because assets placed in these trusts generally don't impact one's eligibility for government assistance.

Because they cannot be revised, using an irrevocable trust during one's lifetime is relatively rare and should be considered cautiously. An irrevocable trust is far more common after one's death, when their specific plan of distribution would control the usage and distribution of the assets.

To Trust or Not to Trust

Trusts serve a valuable function in overall estate planning. They allow assets to pass directly to trust beneficiaries without going through probate, and you can control how your money is managed and distributed to your beneficiaries after you pass. This is particularly valuable if you have any concerns about the spending habits or general behavior of your beneficiaries. Trusts have been very effective when one's children are known to overspend on a regular basis.

In one situation when I served as trustee, the son spent time in and out of jail over the years for drug and alcohol-related issues. In this circumstance, a trust was necessary to keep a considerable sum of money away from someone whose choices may have caused them harm. The trust protected not just the funds but a life!

However, many times, trusts are used unnecessarily when far more cost-effective means of transferring property would have sufficed. Having a lawyer prepare a trust is an expensive undertaking, easily costing several thousand dollars. In contrast, adding a beneficiary to an account or titling a property correctly is free! You need to obtain the correct form, fill it out properly, and sign it. This is a much cheaper option that also avoids probate and controls who gets the asset when you pass.

We often see people fail to utilize the cost-effective and time-saving options that exist under the operation of law or the operation of contract principles discussed previously. Instead, they were convinced they needed to spend a bunch of money on a fifty-page trust when they simply wanted to leave their assets directly to their children and avoid probate. Unfortunately, we see this regularly, and in most cases, it is a waste of money. To be clear, though, if you have concerns over the behavior or decision-making skills of your beneficiaries, then putting some control over your money from the grave by establishing a trust makes sense.

Taxes

Earlier in this book, we partially alluded to Benjamin Franklin's famous quote, again a suitable reminder: *"Nothing is certain except death and taxes."* And sometimes, they show up in combination. Two main types of taxes can apply on a transfer of assets from one person to another: gift taxes and estate taxes.

- **Gift taxes** are payable by the giver on certain transfers made during the giver's lifetime.
- **Estate taxes** (also known as death taxes) are imposed on one's estate after they pass and are based on the total value of that estate's assets.

Lifetime Gift and Estate Tax Exemption

In the U.S., estate and gift taxes are combined into a single unified tax credit, translating to a $12.92 million exemption per individual (for 2023).

This means that during one's lifetime or at death, every person can effectively transfer a total of nearly $13 million in assets without having to pay any estate or gift taxes. In addition, you can also transfer an unlimited amount of assets to your spouse, but this may only postpone taxes as those become due upon the death of the surviving spouse.

Federal estate tax rates are a hefty 40 percent and apply to one's taxable estate, but again, they are offset by a $12.92 million exemption. To calculate the tax owed, take the value of one's assets at death, less any debts, and then subtract $12.92 million (the lifetime exemption). Some states also impose separate estate taxes, up to a maximum of 18 percent on much smaller estates, but fortunately, my home state, Florida, is not one of them!

Today, less than 0.1 percent of all estates pay federal estate taxes, so it typically impacts the super-wealthy. Because of that, it is debated quite frequently by politicians as an area ripe for revenue-raising potential! Currently, the estate tax exemption amount is set to reduce to $5.49 million in 2026, and given the political discussions, we suspect that threshold may decrease even further. In the late 90s, when I started in this business, the estate tax exemption amount was only $650,000! As the taxable threshold amount lowers, we expect an increase in the use of credit shelter and marital trusts to minimize potential estate tax bills as much as possible.

Gifting Exemptions

Most of the transfer tax questions our clients ask involve giving gifts to their families. People often think they must pay taxes when making or receiving a financial or property gift. However, gifts made during one's lifetime rarely trigger any taxes because each person can give any other individual $17,000 per year as of 2023. This is known as the annual gifting exemption and does not include payments made directly to an institution such as your child's college or your parent's medical provider.

Additionally, a married couple can leverage the concept of gift splitting to fully maximize any gift to a friend or family member. For example, if a couple wants to give a gift to their daughter and son-in-law, they could give a combined gift as high as $68,000 (4 x $17,000) in a single year. If any gift or gift split exceeds the applicable maximum exclusion, then one should file a gift tax return and report the excess amount of the gift. One's lifetime $12.92 million estate/gift exemption would then be reduced by this extra amount. Such a gift still won't trigger an immediate tax responsibility, so long as it does not exceed this lifetime exemption.

Cost Basis

A critical distinction between gifting during one's lifetime and transferring property at death involves cost basis treatment for the particular asset. As discussed in Chapter 16, cost basis determines the amount of any gain or loss from the sale of an asset that must be reported on one's tax return. At death, the cost basis for a beneficiary will step up to the value of the asset at the time the person passes, effectively eliminating any tax consequences from the subsequent sale of such assets.

In contrast, when an asset is gifted during one's lifetime, there is no step-up in basis, and the receiver assumes the giver's cost basis. Consequently, if the receiver subsequently sells the gifted asset, then any tax implications are based on the giver's original basis. These rules create a significant distinction in tax treatment between inherited and gifted property.

Proper Estate Planning

Coping with the emotional and financial impact of a loved one's passing can be overwhelming. Having a proper plan in place can help make that transition smoother for your loved ones. Effective estate planning is also essential to ensure that your property is transferred according to your wishes and to minimize any transfer expenses.

A multitude of websites offer relatively quick and cost-effective estate document preparation services. But proceed with caution. If documents aren't completed and executed with complete accuracy, they may be invalid. We recommend limiting the use of these online services to only the simplest of estate plans, like directly leaving all your assets equally to your adult children. For anything that involves more complexity or includes a trust, consult an attorney to ensure your estate plan is in proper order.

Much of the necessary and proper planning can easily be accomplished by the operation of law or the operation of contract concepts discussed earlier in this chapter. By double-checking property titling and named beneficiaries, you can avoid unintended consequences. The bottom line is to take the time to do your homework on planning your estate. Take full advantage of all the available options to pass property to others effectively.

Chapter 20

The Pitfalls of Inheriting Money

I always raise an eyebrow a little bit when someone starts talking about money they plan to inherit. It's usually brought up at the end of our conversation and presented as a magical solution to their financial woes.

"You see, Joel," they say, "my aging parents have money that will be mine, and then things will be great for me financially."

I certainly hope you are not in that category; if you are, please reread the preceding chapters of this book.

Your financial security is yours alone to achieve and should never depend on what may or may not happen in the future. Even if you do inherit money, there are an abundance of considerations, complications, and potential consequences you must understand and evaluate to safeguard your financial security.

The Golden Rule: Don't Assume

A potential inheritance is just that—potential. When it comes to a possible inheritance, my best advice is to prepare to be disappointed. Not only are most inheritances less than people expect, but they can come with a significant number of difficulties and decisions that must be resolved with time, energy, and sometimes additional money.

204 | Next Gen Dollars and Sense

The average inheritance is $46,200, not exactly a life-changing amount. Of those who inherited money between 1980 and 2010, 80 percent received significantly less than they expected.

Never adjust or change your plans until the individual from whom you are expecting an inheritance passes away, their debts are paid in full, all court filings are complete, and the final check is literally in your hand.

Much can happen along the way, particularly with rising end-of-life healthcare costs and evolving estate tax laws. For a somewhat humorous take on what happens when you assume too much, watch the 2022 movie *The Estate,* starring Kathleen Turner and David Duchovny. In the film, multiple family members and potential beneficiaries turn themselves into knots, trying to please their grumpy aunt. In the end, her $18 million estate evaporates to less than $100 because of back taxes and other debts. It's often true that fiction imitates life!

The Pause Button is Your Friend

The loss of a loved one is highly emotional. When combined with a sudden infusion of money, it can be too much to process reasonably. That's why it's essential to take some time and think strategically. The world is full of cautionary tales from lottery winners and professional athletes who instantaneously received significant sums of money and spent it all nearly as fast.

I remember meeting with a family about a decade ago who won more than $100 million in the lottery. When we first met, they explained their elaborate plans for large waterfront mansions with bowling alleys for every member of the family (and it was a large family!). I found myself in the awkward position of explaining that their money would not stretch that far since nearly half of it would be needed for the resulting tax bill. Unfortunately, as is often the case, when we give the advice people need to hear, they often seek out others who are more willing to tell them what they want to hear. I sure hope some of those winnings are still left for that family, but I doubt it.

This point cannot be understated: the combination of losing a loved one and making significant financial decisions creates tremendous stress. It is not a suitable time for big decisions, and it's essential to have enough time to process your emotions and the logistics involved. The process of settling an estate typically takes a minimum of 12 to 18 months, with a multitude of decisions and piles of paperwork. Furthermore, if your spouse has passed, we recommend taking at least a year before making any major life decisions.

Figure Out What You Got

It helps to take adequate time to understand all aspects of the assets you are inheriting. Some property is more liquid than others, like stocks or bonds, which technically can be converted to cash nearly instantaneously to be used for other purposes. However, you may want to assess their current market value to determine if it's a wise financial decision.

Other assets, such as limited partnerships or small businesses, may be entirely illiquid for the foreseeable future. If so, then it's best to learn more about the property and exercise patience while the value is determined correctly. Conversely, assets like investment properties may require your immediate attention to ensure ongoing management and maintenance continues.

It's valuable to step back and evaluate the nature of each asset that you are inheriting and its available options. Not doing so can cost you money in the long run. The reality is that you can't pick and choose what you inherit, and some assets, like cash, are always easier to manage than others, like property. Regardless, there is still actual money involved, and some assets may require effort and patience to resolve the particulars fully!

I saw the financial value of patience in action many years ago when I served as a trustee for a trust that owned a low-income housing real estate limited partnership. These types of investments are highly illiquid, and an individual has no control over the underlying property assets. In this case, the partnership languished for many years and contained a single property in California. The two beneficiaries of this trust were brothers, one of whom lacked patience and disclaimed his share of the investment to his brother. Years later, the remaining brother unexpectedly received a check for nearly $100,000. The last property in the partnership had finally sold and generated a very nice profit. Failure to fully understand and appreciate the assets you inherit can be a costly mistake!

Taxes, Taxes, and More Taxes

You didn't think that this chapter would avoid a discussion about tax implications, did you? By now, you should clearly see that taxes impact almost everything. We'll begin by clarifying what taxes you should expect to pay.

Estate Taxes

Estate taxes are unlikely to apply to most people because of the almost $13 million estate tax exemption discussed in the previous chapter. This means estate taxes will only be due if the decedent's estate is worth more than that amount. If you're facing potential estate tax issues, congratulations are in order: you just inherited a whole lot of money.

Estate taxes are due within nine months of the decedent's passing, but a variety of strategies exist to minimize them, such as various trusts and charitable giving. In these scenarios, we encourage clients to think intergenerationally, including their children, grandchildren, or even older family members. Given the previously discussed expected reduction in the estate tax exemption to much lower levels, we suspect these conversations will increase in the years ahead.

Income Taxes

For the rest of us, the only relevant taxes are income taxes, which depend directly on the nature of the inherited asset. For life insurance, Roth IRAs, bank accounts, CDs, and money markets, there are essentially no tax implications.

Generally, real estate and market assets such as stocks, bonds, or mutual funds are subject to the step-up in cost basis rules previously discussed. The only gain or loss on the sale of those items is based on whether the asset gained or lost value between the date of the decedent's passing and the time such property was sold.

Some tax implications exist for the following assets:

- **Investment Real Estate**: If a property has been used as an investment property, any subsequent sale could include a recapture of any prior depreciation or similar tax write-off on the value of the property.

- **Non-qualified Annuities**: Since these annuities are funded with after-tax dollars, the gain above the original investment is taxable at ordinary income tax rates.

- **Qualified Annuities:** These treated as IRAs and are subject to very specific rules (detailed in Chapter 17) involving the period that the account balance must be fully distributed and income taxes paid in their entirety. In addition, insurance companies often impose a payout schedule on annuities.

Income Taxes on Traditional IRAs

Traditional IRAs are the most taxable and complicated type of asset to inherit. Prior to 2020, inheriting an IRA was more straightforward, as beneficiaries could stretch out the required minimum distributions over the course of their lifetime. This stretch feature was a compelling option, allowing you to withdraw a minimal amount each year and leave the remaining balance growing on a tax-deferred basis.

I remember one situation about a decade ago when a ten-year-old grandchild inherited an IRA of nearly $500,000. The required annual distribution amounted to about 3 percent, or $15,000 each year, and was subject to the youngster's very low tax bracket. Meanwhile, the remaining balance of the inherited IRA stayed invested and continued to grow on a tax-deferred basis. At last count, the inherited IRA balance had grown to about $750,000 over the ensuing decade and should continue to grow tax-deferred for the rest of the now twenty-year-old's lifetime. This stretch feature presented a fantastic opportunity for tax-deferred generational wealth.

Unfortunately, as discussed in Chapter 17, the stretch IRA no longer exists. After 2020, the maximum stretch period was significantly reduced to ten years, fundamentally changing the tax implications of inheriting an IRA. The new rules stipulate that the entire balance of the account must be distributed (and taxes paid) within a maximum of ten years. While this provision gives beneficiaries some flexibility, proper planning is critical to managing the distribution sequence and its resulting tax implications. For example, if you plan to retire in four years and inherit an IRA, one strategy is to leave the account alone for the first four years while you are still working and then evenly spread the distribution of the remaining balance over the next six years. As you can imagine, proper planning in this case is imperative to minimize taxes.

What's Your Financial Picture?

Once you have a handle on the amount, nature, and tax implications of your inheritance, it's time to integrate this into your personal financial situation. Start by revisiting your financial goals and asking yourself these key questions.

- **Were you on track for retirement?** If not, does the amount you inherited get you back on track, or do you still have work to do? Remember, most inheritances aren't very sizable, so while it may help somewhat, you must view this as an opportunity to focus on your personal financial efforts and future plans.

- **Do you have outstanding debt to address?** Paying off unsecured or high-interest debt with an inheritance is a sound decision. Eliminating such debt improves your cash flow, which creates an opportunity to boost your regular savings.

- **Does your personal estate plan need to be revised?** With this new influx of money, your own plan may need to be revisited.

- **Does this money impact your diversification?** Or are there areas that got out of balance, and these funds now provide an opportunity to rebalance your existing investments? Inheriting money is an opportune time to revisit your current investment allocation. Investing any amount of money, whether inherited or not, requires its own specifically tailored mix and approach.

- **Do you have a regular investing plan yet?** After deciding on the proper allocation considering your current investment mix, one of the best approaches to investing a sum of money is to do so in portions at regular intervals over time.

This dollar-cost averaging approach we discussed in Chapter 13 is a great way to integrate your inherited money with your existing investments.

- **What about including a charity that your loved one especially appreciated?** This option is a great way to honor someone and continue their memory for years to come. When my sister-in-law passed away unexpectedly, some of her money was used to fund various art ventures that she was particularly fond of at her alma mater.

The bottom line is that there is much more to inheriting money than simply cashing a check. Proper care and planning are critical, and more so when wealth transfers from one person to another. The reality is that over the next 20 years, the world will see the greatest wealth transfer from one generation to the next in all of human history. The need to be prepared with a game plan for that is paramount.

Chapter 21

Dollars and Sense

Dollars & Sense is not only in this book's title but also the name of our long-running radio show and podcast. The About the Author section contains a description of the show and a variety of ways to find and subscribe to the weekly broadcast. After nearly 1,500 episodes, we still haven't run out of topics to share with our listeners.

Every decade of life is different as you age, and your financial objectives should change accordingly. Being on the right track toward a successful retirement requires accomplishing certain milestones. This chapter summarizes the concepts introduced throughout this book and outlines which ones to focus on at different ages.

Goals for Your Twenties

In your twenties, you have an excellent opportunity to establish good financial habits that can set you up for success in the long term. The sooner you start working toward your goals, the more likely you are to achieve them. Here are some financial goals you should consider working on in your twenties:

- **Establish a Budget.** Creating a budget will help you manage your money and ensure you live

211

within your means. It can also help identify where you can cut back on expenses to save money for the future.

- **Pay Off High-Interest Debt.** If you have any high-interest debt, such as credit cards, pay it off promptly. The interest charges on high-interest debt add up over time and drag down your finances significantly.

- **Build an Emergency Fund.** Start building an emergency fund to cover at least three to six months of living expenses. This provides a financial cushion for unexpected events like losing your job or facing a medical emergency.

- **Start Saving for Retirement.** Even though retirement may seem a long way off, it's never too early to start saving. Contribute to an IRA or a 401(k), especially if your employer offers a matching contribution. Your investment allocation should be highly growth-oriented and focus predominantly on stocks.

- **Build Credit.** Establishing good credit can help you qualify for lower interest rates on mortgages, credit cards, and insurance premiums. Always pay your bills on time, keep your credit utilization low, and avoid opening too many new accounts at once.

- **Invest in Yourself.** Investing in additional education or job skills can help increase your income over time. This can include taking courses, attending conferences, or pursuing certifications relevant to your career—some of which your employer may even be willing to pay for.

Goals for Your Thirties

In your thirties, you should continue building on the financial foundation established in your twenties and add on these financial objectives to gain further traction:

- **Increase Your Emergency Fund.** By your thirties, aim for an emergency fund covering at least six to nine months of living expenses. This will provide you with a more substantial financial cushion in case of unexpected events.

- **Pay Off All Non-Mortgage Debt.** If you still have non-mortgage debt, such as student or car loans, pay it off as soon as possible. This frees up more money for other financial goals, such as retirement savings or a home down payment.

- **Maximize Your Retirement Contributions.** By your thirties, aim to contribute at least 10 percent of your income to retirement savings. If you have been putting your salary increases into savings over the years, you should already be close to that 10 percent. Take full advantage of the tax benefits from retirement contributions and any available employer matching. Continue using a highly growth-oriented investment allocation and start interviewing financial professionals you can rely on for financial guidance.

- **Save for a Downpayment on a Home.** If you plan to buy a home, start saving for a downpayment. Save at least 20 percent of the home's purchase price to avoid private mortgage insurance (PMI) and lower your monthly payments. The average age of a first-time homebuyer is thirty-six, so acquiring a home in your thirties puts you on track financially.

- **Review Your Insurance Coverage.** Ensure you have adequate insurance coverage, including health, life, disability, umbrella, and homeowner's or renter's insurance. Consider increasing your coverage if your financial situation has changed since you last reviewed your policies.

- **Create an Estate Plan.** To ensure your assets are distributed according to your wishes in case of your unexpected death, take the time to create a will and execute the proper estate planning documents. Check the beneficiaries on your accounts to ensure the correct individuals are listed. These steps can help your family and beneficiaries avoid probate and minimize taxes.

Goals for Your Forties

In your forties, you are likely approaching the prime point of your career and have more significant earning potential than in your twenties and thirties. Here are some key financial goals to accomplish in your forties:

- **Increase Your Retirement Savings.** By your forties, you should contribute even more to your retirement savings. Increase your contribution rate from 10 to 15 percent, and try to invest the maximum allowable amount in a 401(k) or IRA.

- **Review Your Investment Portfolio.** Ensure your investment portfolio aligns with your long-term financial goals and risk tolerance. Consider rebalancing your portfolio, if necessary, and start regularly consulting a financial professional to help achieve your financial plans. While still growth-oriented, your investment allocation should not be as aggressive as it was in your twenties and thirties.

- **Develop a Strategy to Pay off Your Mortgage in the Next Ten to Fifteen Years.** Consider making extra payments to pay off your mortgage before you retire. Being mortgage-free can provide increased financial stability and flexibility in the long run, especially in retirement.

- **Save for Your Children's Education.** If you have children, start saving for their college education. Use a 529 plan or other tax-advantaged savings account to maximize your investments.

- **Evaluate Your Career and Earning Potential.** Explore opportunities to advance your career or increase your earning potential. This might include pursuing additional education or training, seeking a promotion, or starting a business.

Goals for Your Fifties

In your fifties, you are likely in the prime of your career, with retirement approaching. According to a recent study, financial literacy typically peaks at age fifty-four when your expertise and cognition align to produce better financial decisions. Here are some financial milestones to achieve in your fifties:

- **Maximize Your Retirement Savings.** By your fifties, you should contribute the maximum amount to your retirement accounts, such as a 401(k) or IRA. Increase your contributions to take advantage of the applicable catch-up contribution amounts that are available over the age of fifty. This helps you achieve your retirement goals and take advantage of the related tax benefits.

- **Pay Off All Mortgage Debt.** Aim to pay off all mortgage debt, along with any other debts outstanding. This will free up cash to focus on your retirement goals.

- **Evaluate Your Retirement Readiness.** With retirement approaching, evaluate whether you're on target to meet your retirement objectives. Consult with a financial professional regularly to review your retirement savings progress and potential income sources. At this point, your investment allocation should gradually shift to a more growth and income strategy.

- **Consider Downsizing.** If you own a large home and the children have moved out, consider downsizing to a smaller home or more affordable area to reduce your housing expenses and free up cash for other financial goals.

- **Plan for Healthcare Costs.** As you age, healthcare costs can become a significant expense. Be sure to start budgeting for out-of-pocket healthcare costs.

- **Review Your Estate Plan.** Make sure your estate plan is up-to-date and reflects your wishes. Examine your will, trust, and named beneficiaries to ensure they are still appropriate.

Let's Get Started!

No matter where you are in your financial journey, the first step toward achieving your goals is understanding your financial situation. Here is a recap of steps to understand your current financial situation better and plan for your future:

- **Calculate Your Net Worth.** Your net worth is the difference between your assets (what you own) and your liabilities (what you owe). This provides a snapshot of your current financial situation. Many online calculators and tools exist to help calculate your net worth, including the one provided in Chapter 4. Remember to save this calculation each year to track your financial progress! A direct link to our Net Worth Worksheet can be found on the book's website at www.NextGenDollarsAndSense.com or by scanning the QR code below.

Net Worth Worksheet

- **Review Your Budget.** A budget is essential for tracking income and expenses. Review your budget to see where your money goes each month and identify where you can cut back on costs or increase savings. Use the approach described in Chapter 4 or scan the QR code below for our Budget Template, which is also available at www.NextGenDollarsAndSense.com.

Budget Tracker

- **Review Your Credit Report.** Your credit report contains information about your credit history and is used by lenders to determine your creditworthiness. Review your credit report to ensure there are no errors or fraudulent activity. Take steps to improve your credit score with the techniques discussed in Chapter 6.

- **Identify Your Financial Goals.** Think about what you'd like to achieve financially in the short and long term. This could include saving for retirement, paying off debt, or buying a home. Identify your financial goals and prioritize them based on their importance using the steps we outlined in Chapter 3.

- **Meet with a Financial Planner Who is an Experienced Fiduciary.** Consider meeting with a financial planner who can help you review your financial situation and create a customized financial plan. A financial planner can provide valuable insights and recommendations on achieving your financial goals and creating a personalized plan. Ensure they are a fiduciary, either a CERTIFIED FINANCIAL PLANNING™ Professional or a Certified Financial Fiduciary®. A fiduciary is required to advise in a manner that benefits you, not them.

Reach Out to Learn More

Contact Information

If you would like to set up a free conversation with our team at Nelson Financial Planning, please contact us:

- Call: 407-629-6477
- Email Joel@NelsonFinancialPlanning.com
- Online: www.NelsonFinancialPlanning.com

Subscribe to *Dollars & Sense*

Our radio show/podcast provides weekly updates on the latest economic and financial changes. You can subscribe on your favorite podcast platform or the Nelson Financial Planning YouTube channel. The following About the Author section features a variety of QR codes that will help you directly connect with us.

Questions & Notes

About the Author

Joel J. Garris is the President and Chief Executive Officer of Nelson Financial Planning, Inc., and enjoys helping people achieve their financial goals. He provides financial planning guidance to families, businesses, and individuals about taxes, retirement, and investments and specializes in bringing perspective to life's financial decisions. His areas of expertise include income planning, wealth management, legacy planning, and minimizing taxes.

Joel is a CERTIFIED FINANCIAL PLANNER™ Professional, Certified Financial Fiduciary®, and holds various securities licenses, including:

- Series 7—General Securities Representative
- Series 24—General Securities Principal
- Series 27/28—Financial and Operations Principal
- Series 51—Municipal Fund Securities Principal

A graduate of Boston University School of Law, he is a former member of the Massachusetts and Washington, DC bars.

He can be reached at (407) 629-6477
or Joel@NelsonFinancialPlanning.com

Joel is the current host of one of Central Florida's longest-running radio shows, which was started in 1984 by his father-in-law, Jack Nelson. *Dollars & Sense* airs live every Sunday throughout Central Florida:

- 9:00 a.m. to 10:00 a.m. on WFLA 93.1FM / 540 AM
- 9:00 a.m. to 10:00 a.m. on The Game 96.9 FM
- 11:00 a.m. to 12:00 p.m. on WMMB 92.7 FM

Recently named one of the Top 25 Financial Planning Podcasts by Feedspot, the show is available on numerous podcast platforms and its YouTube channel.

Previously, Joel was the host of "Moneywise," a financial call-in talk show on WORL 660 AM, and taught a personal enrichment class entitled *Analyzing and Solving Life's Financial Matters* through Orange County Public Schools. Joel has been interviewed on a variety of radio programs, including National Public Radio and Good Morning Orlando. His television appearances include national content provider Ivanhoe Broadcasting and "Best of Central Florida" on CBS affiliate WKMG.

Joel served as an Assistant Scoutmaster for Troop 24, chartered by First Presbyterian Church of Orlando, and has been a youth sports coach for Delaney Park Little League, Association of Christian Youth Sports, YMCA, and Upward. He is also a member of various organizations, including Mensa, and has been a volunteer for Literacy Volunteers of America and the Veterans' Administration.

Joel and his wife Stephanie will celebrate their 25th anniversary in 2024. Stephanie is President and CEO of Grace Medical Home, a non-profit that provides medical care for the uninsured. She is also a past President of the Junior League of Greater Orlando. Their oldest son, Nelson, is a recent graduate of Auburn University, their middle son, Ethan, is pursuing a master's degree in accounting at the University of Virginia, and their youngest son, Connor, is studying at Northeastern University. All three are graduates of Boone High School and The Christ School in downtown Orlando.

Dollars & Sense is our weekly podcast and radio show that provides timely updates on the markets, the headlines, and the economy.

As one of Central Florida's longest-running radio shows, it is also a Top 25 Financial Planning Podcast with regular downloads averaging over 1,000 per month.

Hosted by Joel Garris and the team of Certified Financial Fiduciaries at Nelson Financial Planning, the show helps you make sense out of all of life's decisions involving your dollars. Be sure to subscribe to our channel on any of the platforms below and on the following page to receive updates when new content is posted.

9:00 AM

11:00 AM

Spotify

Apple Podcasts

Facebook

Twitter

SoundCloud

iHeart Radio

Notes and Sources

Chapter 1 Human Behavior

1. Wadley, Jared. "Study Looks at Responses to Negative, Positive News" The University Record, n.d. https://record.umich.edu/articles/study-looks-at-responses-to-negative-positive-news/.

2. Barber, Brad & Odean, Terrance. (2008). All That Glitters: The Effect of Attention and News on the Buying Behavior of Individual and Institutional Investors. Review of Financial Studies. 21. 785-818. 10.2139/ssrn.460660.

3. Naurin, Elin, Stuart Soroka, and Niels Markwat. "Asymmetric Accountability: An Experimental Investigation of Biases in Evaluations of Governments' Election Pledges." Comparative Political Studies 52, no. 13–14 (March 14, 2019): 2207–34. https://doi.org/10.1177/0010414019830740.

4. "The American College of Financial Services," n.d. https://www.theamericancollege.edu/.

5. Magellan Financial Group 2019. https://www.magellangroup.com.au/.

6. The Decision Lab. "Anchoring Bias - The Decision Lab," n.d. https://thedecisionlab.com/biases/anchoring-bias/.

7. Inman, Mary. "Hindsight Bias | Definition, Psychology, & Examples." Encyclopedia Britannica, August 18, 2023. https://www.britannica.com/topic/hindsight-bias.

8. "Status Quo Bias" The BE Hub. BehavioralEconomics.com | The BE Hub, February 20, 2023. https://www.behavioraleconomics.com/resources/mini-encyclopedia-of-be/status-quo-bias/.

9. "Definition of Bandwagon Effect." In *Merriam-Webster Dictionary*, July 8, 2023. https://www.merriam-webster.com/dictionary/bandwagon%20effect.
10. Dalbar, 2023 QAIB Report, as of December 31, 2022
11. Dickler, Jessica. "Strategies to Navigate the $68 Trillion 'Great Wealth Transfer,' According to Top-Ranked Advisors." *CNBC*, October 17, 2022. https://www.cnbc.com/2022/10/17/how-to-navigate-the-great-wealth-transfer-according-to-top-advisors.html.

Chapter 2 The Fundamentals

1. Isaacson, Walter. "The Real Leadership Lessons of Steve Jobs." Harvard Business Review, October 29, 2014. https://hbr.org/2012/04/the-real-leadership-lessons-of-steve-jobs.
2. Putnam Investments. "Time, not timing, is the best way to capitalize on stock market gains" Putnam Investments | 100 Federal Street | Boston, MA 02110 | Putnam.com.
3. Hogan, Chris. Ramsey Solutions. *Everyday Millionaires: How Ordinary People Built Extraordinary Wealth–and How You Can Too*, 2019.

Chapter 4 Net Worth, Budgeting Basics, and Emergency Savings

1. Kerr, Emma. "10 Most Common Budgeting Mistakes (and How to Fix Them)." *US News & World Report*, June 30, 2022. https://money.usnews.com/money/personal-finance/slideshows/8-big-budgeting-blunders-and-how-to-fix-them.
2. Ceravolo, Maria Gabriella, Mara Fabri, Lucrezia Fattobene, Gabriele Polonara, and GianMario Raggetti. "Cash, Card or Smartphone: The Neural Correlates of Payment Methods." *Frontiers in Neuroscience* 13 (November 5, 2019). https://doi.org/10.3389/fnins.2019.01188.

Chapter 5 Managing Debt

1. "Fiscal Data Explains the National Debt," n.d. https://fiscaldata.treasury.gov/americas-finance-guide/national-debt/.
2. Hoover Institution. "The US Debt—Causes and Consequences," n.d. https://www.hoover.org/research/us-debt-causes-and-consequences-0.
3. Sato, Gayle. "Secured vs. Unsecured Loans: What You Need to Know." *www.experian.com*, October 15, 2020. https://www.experian.com/blogs/ask-experian/secured-vs-unsecured-loans-what-you-should-know/.
4. Taylor, Mia. "Pros and Cons of Debt Consolidation." *Bankrate*, August 23, 2023. https://www.bankrate.com/personal-finance/debt/pros-and-cons-of-debt-consolidation/.

Chapter 6 Credit and Your Credit Score

1. Team, Cfi. "Types of Credit." *Corporate Finance Institute*, December 11, 2022. https://corporatefinanceinstitute.com/resources/commercial-lending/types-of-credit/.
2. Equifax. "How Are Credit Scores Calculated?" *Equifax*, 2018. https://www.equifax.com/personal/education/credit/score/how-is-credit-score-calculated/.
3. VanSomeren, Lindsay. "9 Benefits Of Good Credit And How It Can Help You Financially." *Forbes Advisor*, July 21, 2021. https://www.forbes.com/advisor/credit-score/benefits-of-good-credit/.
4. "Your Rights to Your Free Annual Credit Reports - Annual Credit Report.Com.," n.d. https://www.annualcreditreport.com/yourRights.action.

Chapter 7 Stocks

1. "Dow Jones Average | Definition, History, & Facts Definition | Britannica Money," n.d. https://www.britannica.com/money/Dow-Jones-average.

2. S&P Dow Jones Indices. "S&P 500®," n.d. https://www.spglobal.com/spdji/en/indices/equity/sp-500/#overview.

3. Nasdaq. "Historical Data," n.d. https://www.nasdaq.com/market-activity/quotes/historical.

4. Hargrave, Marshall. "Standard Deviation Formula and Uses vs. Variance." Investopedia, May 11, 2023. https://www.investopedia.com/terms/s/standarddeviation.asp.

5. "Alphabet Announces Second Quarter 2022 Results Document," n.d. https://www.sec.gov/Archives/edgar/data/1652044/000165204422000068/googexhibit991q22022.htm.

6. Arrieche, Alejandro. "Microsoft Shareholders: Who Owns the Most MSFT Stock?" *Capital Com SV Investments Limited,* November 16, 2022. https://capital.com/microsoft-shareholder-who-owns-most-msft-stock.

7. Investment Company Institute. "The US ETF Market: FAQs," April 10, 2023. https://www.ici.org/faqs/faq/etfs/faqs_etfs_market.

8. Statista. "Total Active and Passive Mutual Funds in the U.S. 2000-2022." Statista, June 13, 2023. https://www.statista.com/statistics/1263885/number-active-passive-mutual-funds-usa.

Chapter 8 Bonds

1. Macroaxis LLC (www.macroaxis.com). "Microsoft 2023 Bonds | NASDAQ(MSFT)." Macroaxis, n.d. https://www.macroaxis.com/invest/bond/.

2. U.S. Department of The Treasury. "Interest Rate Statistics," August 28, 2023. https://home.treasury.gov/policy-issues/financing-the-government/interest-rate-statistics.

Chapter 9 Mutual Funds

1. Morningstar, Inc. "Morningstar Ratings 101," n.d. https://www.morningstar.com/company/morningstar-ratings-faq.

Chapter 10 Annuities

1. Greenberg, Gregg. "Record Annuity Sales in 2022 Could Very Well Continue into 2023." InvestmentNews, July 12, 2023. https://www.investmentnews.com/annuity-industry-eyes-another-record-year-2022s-sales-237528.
2. McGonigal, Caitlyn. "High Interest Rates, Aging Americans Driving Record Demand for Annuities into 2027." *Annuity.Org*, August 27, 2023. https://www.annuity.org/2023/08/19/high-interest-rates-aging-americans-driving-record-demand-for-annuities-into-2027/.
3. Ramsey, Dave. "What Is an Annuity and How Does It Work?" *Ramsey Solutions*, September 6, 2023. https://www.ramseysolutions.com/retirement/what-is-annuity.
4. Annuity Digest. "Buffett Blasts Life Insurers for Taking on Crazy Risks with Variable Annuity Guarantees | Annuity Digest," n.d. https://www.annuitydigest.com/blog/tom/buffett-blasts-life-insurers-taking-crazy-risks-variable-annuity-guarantees.

Chapter 11 Rates of Return and the Economic Cycle

1. Capital Group EACG. "How Long Do Recessions Last," n.d. https://www.capitalgroup.com/.
2. Putnam Investments. "Markets recover from crises," n.d. https://www.putnam.com/.
3. Team, Investopedia. "Which Investments Have the Highest Historical Returns?" *Investopedia*, September 29, 2022. https://www.investopedia.com/ask/answers/032415/which-investments-have-highest-historical-returns.asp.

Chapter 12 Asset Allocation

1. Neufeld, Dorothy. "Visualizing 90 Years of Stock and Bond Portfolio Performance." Visual Capitalist, March 23, 2023. https://www.visualcapitalist.com/90-years-stock-and-bond-portfolio-performance/.

Chapter 13 The Average Person's DIY Results

1. MFS® Investments. "Average Investor Underperformed," https://www.mfs.com/.
2. Putnam Investments. "Stay invested so you don't miss the markets best days" Putnam Investments | 100 Federal Street | Boston, MA 02110 | Putnam.com.

Chapter 14 Life's Big Purchases

1. "What Is a Mortgage?" *Bankrate*, August 9, 2023. https://www.bankrate.com/mortgages/what-is-mortgage/#what-is-included.
2. Hardesty, Chris. "How To Beat Car Depreciation - Kelley Blue Book." Kelley Blue Book, September 11, 2023. https://www.kbb.com/car-advice/how-to-beat-car-depreciation/.

Chapter 15 College Planning

1. "Federal Student Aid," n.d. https://studentaid.gov/understand-aid/types/loans/interest-rates.

Chapter 16 Taxes

1. Fíonta and Fíonta. "How Many Words Are in the Tax Code?" *Tax Foundation*, July 24, 2023. https://taxfoundation.org/how-many-words-are-tax-code.
2. "IRA Deduction Limits | Internal Revenue Service," n.d. https://www.irs.gov/retirement-plans/ira-deduction-limits.
3. "Tax Code, Regulations, and Official Guidance | Internal Revenue Service," n.d. https://www.irs.gov/privacy-disclosure/tax-code-regulations-and-official-guidance.

4. "Here's a Quick Overview of Tax Reform Changes and Where Taxpayers Can Find More Info | Internal Revenue Service," n.d. https://www.irs.gov/newsroom/heres-a-quick-overview-of-tax-reform-changes-and-where-taxpayers-can-find-more-info.

5. "Life of Tax: How Much Tax Is Paid Over a Lifetime | Self." www.Self.Inc, March 28, 2023. https://www.self.inc/info/life-of-tax.

Chapter 17 Retirement Accounts

1. "Topic No. 404, Dividends | Internal Revenue Service," n.d. https://www.irs.gov/taxtopics/tc404.

2. myFRS. "MyFRS," n.d. https://www.myfrs.com/.

Chapter 18 Social Security

1. "Social Security History," n.d. https://www.ssa.gov/history/ratios.html.

Chapter 19 Death: The Other Certainty

1. "Estate Tax | Internal Revenue Service," n.d. https://www.irs.gov/businesses/small-businesses-self-employed/estate-tax.

Chapter 20 The Pitfalls of Inheriting Money

1. "Gift Tax | Internal Revenue Service," n.d. https://www.irs.gov/businesses/small-businesses-self-employed/gift-tax.

2. Marsano, John. "Inheritance Statistics In 2023 | Inheritance Advanced." *Inheritance Advanced* (blog), June 22, 2023. https://inheritanceadvanced.com/blog/inheritance-statistics.

Chapter 21 Dollars and Sense

1. Ansberry, Clare. "The Exact Age When You Make Your Best Financial Decisions." *WSJ*, August 27, 2023.

https://www.wsj.com/personal-finance/the-exact-age-when-you-make-your-best-financial-decisions.

2. www.nar.realtor. "Share of First-Time Buyers Smaller, Older than in Past," November 2, 2022. https://www.nar.realtor/newsroom/nar-finds-share-of-first-time-home-buyers-smaller-older-than-ever-before.